The Seneschals of Dol

Also by E.J. Stewart

The Seneschals of Dol

Histories and Mysteries of the Stewart Clan

Jan Eylander Jackson Stewart

Leaf & Vine Books

San Francisco

Published by Leaf & Vine Books
387 Ivy Street
San Francisco, CA 94102

ISBN: 978-0-978-60875-0

Printed in the United States of America.

For
Annabelle Grace Taylor
Alaina Katherine Taylor
Christopher Wren Stewart
etc.

Contents

Foreword

After our grandson Christopher was born, my wife Misa suggested that I rewrite my parents' autobiographies so he would not forget his origins. The suggestion was good, but I could not bring myself to alter their writings. What's more (or what's less, in this case), they were limited in what they could find by their ability to drive throughout the country, visiting relatives and graves, to find what they could find. In today's world we have the Internet, which affords us so much more.

I must admit I was amazed at the result. I knew that my grandmother's family traced their roots back to New Amsterdam, but my father's book only traced our paternal ancestors back four generations, to North Carolina. My mother's family could be traced about the same number of generations, to some obscure forefathers in Ireland.

In the end, there is one observation that holds true. Every person who is born with the family name *Stewart* descends from the same person – every last one of us. That person is Walter FitzAlan, the first High Steward of Scotland (ca. 1106-1178). He came from France, a scion of the Seneschals of Dol, in Brittany.

One problem with writing a book of ancestry is that this genre is usually so boring that one cannot read more than one or two pages without putting it down and turning on the TV. My parents' books are "imminently readable," but they ramble on and on with many diversions and no chapter divisions, making it difficult to follow the narrative. For this reason, I have chosen to write first-person narratives after the manner of Edgar Lee Masters' classic *Spoon River Anthology*. Admittedly there are gaps in the narratives, which I had to fill in with fictional information (sorry for fudging on history).

I hope you enjoy this little tome. Maybe one day you'll write your own story. I'm sure it will be a good one.

1

Alexander Stewart

1634-1731

"War is Hell," as the saying goes, but in my case it may have been Heaven-sent. That's not to say I enjoyed it. Looking back on the outcome, though, I must say that the war brought changes to my life, changes that I could never have wrought on my own, nor could I have imagined in my wildest dreams.

They called it the English Civil War, but it was the Irish and the Scots who suffered the most. "Us versus Them," if you will. Hadn't we suffered enough? The Highlanders had done most of the fighting up to that point, but little by little they were depleted, until the weight of the battles fell upon us Lowlanders, the residents of Edinburgh and other cities. Now we had to face the facts: Cromwell hadn't come to Dunbar to play golf!

The Presbyterian leadership brought this upon us. It's good to be religious, but those people were just too much! They had even punished one of their own clergymen for playing golf at Dunbar. Now they had relieved some 3,000 of our soldiers of their duties for "moral" offenses such as spitting or swearing.

This time we had Cromwell cornered on the golf course with no escape. The Elders came and said we had to attack, but not on Sunday, because it wasn't a very Godly thing to do. So they made us leave our high position on Doon Hill (we could have just waited for Cromwell's army to starve) and get ready to fight the next day (after a hearty breakfast, of course)!

I never had that hearty breakfast. In fact, it would be seven years before I would have breakfast again at my own table. Cromwell's army attacked us in the middle of the night like a bunch of wild Indians. His roundheads came right into our camp, and chaos broke out. I never knew what hit me… as soon as I ran out of our tent I got smacked on the back of the head with something, probably the stock of a musket. While I was passed out Cromwell sicced his cavalry, "Ironsides" as he called them, on us. It was over in an hour or so.

In all, more than ten thousand prisoners were taken. Cromwell's army couldn't manage that many people, so they let the sick and wounded go. As for the rest of us, we had to march south, more than one hundred twenty miles, past Newcastle to Durham Cathedral. It took us a week. Half of our number either escaped or died during the journey. The rest of us holed up in that cathedral, freezing and starving, burning what we could pry loose from the floor to keep ourselves warm.

The only thing we did not burn was the clock. Maybe it was the majesty of it; maybe the

Scottish Thistle carved at the top. Anyway, it stood there like an ancient oaken deity, ticking out the quarter hours – for some the last quarter hour of their lives – for others, the only thing that reminded us we were still alive. Thirty or forty men died each day. We had to bury them in a trench, but we never filled it in; we just kept adding bodies to it.

One day my "salvation" came. About a hundred and fifty of us were sold into slavery. The slave traders paid £5 each for us, loaded us onto the "good" ship *Unity*, and headed off to the New World. *Unity* – the irony of that name! We had been chained together like dogs! Now we were packed together like sardines! What would become of me? Would I ever see my father again? (There was another lad named Duncan on the ship with us, but his presence there only made me sadder.) What about my beloved Scotland? Oh, for a pint o' bitter at the White Hart Inn!

We lost more of our number to scurvy after we set sail from England. Poor souls. They were buried at sea, for the fish to devour them. Only about sixty of us survived the trip. I was seasick nearly the entire way, so I was relieved, though somewhat apprehensive, when we finally spotted land in December. So this was it? This was the fabled Plymouth Colony that all of England raved about?

Some thirty-five of my fellow prisoners were sent to work in the Hammersmith Ironworks up in Saugus. As for me, I was assigned to Mr. Willoughby's Shipyard in Charlestown. Which was worse, stoking a fire and hauling off slag, or lifting timbers and caulking hulls? More irony – this was the place where the *Unity* was built!

When you are sixteen, being twenty-four seems like being a very old man – one step from Methuselah, so to speak. That's how old I was when I finally wriggled out of this mess. You see, we were Christian slaves, and according to the laws of chivalry, and the ideals of Logres, we could only be held for seven years. After that, we were free to return home or remain as citizens.

It was the Year of Our Lord sixteen hundred and fifty-eight, and I was put out on the streets with no money to buy passage home, no family to turn to… nothing. Luckily, Mr. Richard Templar, a man I had met at the shipyard, took a liking to me and helped me set up a tailoring shop in Charlestown.

Actually, he had other plans for me, as well. You see, his daughter had taken a liking to me, too. So it was that in 1662 I married Hannah Templar and settled down to a new life in Massachusetts Bay Colony, never to return to my beloved Scotland again.

We started a family. Our children were James ('65), **John** ('67), Samuel ('69), Hannah('72) and Margaret ('74): all fine children. Sadly, my wife Hannah died in 1674, when she was thirty-one. We laid her to rest in the Phipps Street Burying Ground in Charlestown.*

* Author's Note: It is one of my greatest regrets that I did not visit Hannah's grave when we went to Boston in 2017. I had not at that time done any research on this subject, so I had no idea that I would have any family there.

After Hannah died, I was called to fight in the Indian war. I couldn't take care of my children, so Hannah's mother offered to help. Happily her new husband, old Mr. Morton, agreed. I guess because his uncle, William Bradford, had taken him in when *his* father died, he wanted to help someone out in return. So my children went out to their new lives on Cape Cod Bay.

The Indians' leader called himself King Philip. They had been attacking our people right and left, so we finally decided to end their campaign of terror. It was ironic that one of their own, a praying Indian named John Alderman, was the one who killed King Philip at Mount Hope. Sadly, we heard that Hannah's little uncle Robert was killed in the fighting up at Saco, Maine.

2

Dr. John Stewart

1667-1765

You may be wondering how I became a doctor. That's a good question, seeing as how there were no medical schools in Plimoth Colony, nor in Massachusetts Bay. The nearest college was a thousand miles away (as the crow flies), in Edinburgh. The next closest college was just as far (as the sea serpent crawls), in Leiden. So how did I do it?

I had a very unhappy childhood. When I was only two, Grandad Templar died. A few years later, Momma joined him. Dad couldn't raise us five kids, so he sent us all to live with Grammie. By that time she had married Mr. Nathaniel Morton, who lived out in Yarmouth. (Their families knew each other when they lived in Leiden, so after their spouses died, they married.)

Mr. Morton was the secretary of Plimoth Colony, and he had gotten a book from the widow of Deacon Samuel Fuller, a preacher who came over on the *Mayflower*.* It was called *The Svrgion's Mate,* by Dr. John Woodall. I read and re-read that book until I had memorized every page. At first I practiced on cats and dogs; after a while I graduated to livestock. By the time I was eighteen, I had my first human case – a little girl who had broken her arm. I used some barrel staves to make splints for her arm – and I was on my way to a brilliant career!

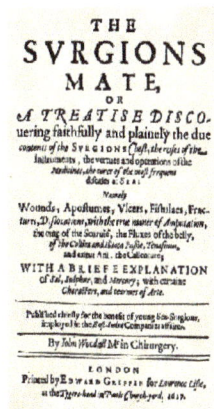

THE
SVRGIONS
MATE,
OR
A TREATISE DISCO.
uering faithfully and plainely the due

---

* Author's Note: Nathaniel Morton delivered the eulogy at Fuller's funeral. By the way Fuller's wife, Jane Lathrop, though not related to the Stewarts at all, had a very interesting background. Her ancestors included Charlemagne, Alfred the Great, William I of England, Hugh Capet, Henry II of England, and some from the Byzantine Empire.

An Apparition

So why did I move to New York? It was a stroke of luck (both good and bad). Bear with me, and I will explain. Just as lightning had struck seven men dead in Boston, in this my nineteenth year I was struck "alive" by a thunderbolt from God, by the voice of His own spirit to my soul. In a waking dream I saw an apparition, the wraith of Joseph of Arimathea, standing at Glastonbury. "Behold the New Jerusalem," he said. Being young at heart and foolish of spirit, I couldn't help but shout the news. What a mistake! The governor would surely have had me dunked (those fanatics in Salem were getting more and more obsessed with witches), for I was a heretic... a Presbyterian at that, and not a Puritan, so I had to leave Plimoth.

I went to minister to the sick in Rhode Island, out to the west of Yarmouth. One patient, a Mr. John Cole, and his wife Susanna had moved there from Boston. His wife, who was about the same age as my father, had a very interesting story to tell.

Mrs. Cole, who was born in England, came to the colonies with her mother, Anne Hutchinson. Mrs. Hutchinson began preaching that some people received revelation from God, and therefore they could know God's will directly. This threatened the Puritans' role as interpreters of the Bible, so they put her on trial and banished her from the colony.

She and her followers fled to the Providence Plantations, but Mr. Winthrop sent his ministers, who told her that Massachusetts would soon take over Rhode Island, so they moved again to New Amsterdam. There Mrs. Hutchinson was attacked by Indians and axed to death.*

During that dastardly attack her daughter Susanna, who had been picking berries, tried to hide in a tree. The savage chief found her and took her away, forcing her to bear him a son, an Indian named John White. A few years later the Dutch noticed her blue eyes and ransomed her, returning her to her older brothers in Boston. Later she married Mr. Cole.

I am "Reborn"

Mrs. Cole put me into contact with her Indian son, who knew of another kidnapped Englishman in what was now New York. 'Twas my good fortune he was named... John Stewart! His father was a nobleman in Scotland who would gladly have paid his ransom, but this poor fellow succumbed to disease. The Indians had not told the Europeans. That is how I was able to assume his identity. In a sense I was "re-born"... as myself, but seven years older!

That is how I established myself on the Long Island precinct of Queens, safely out of the reach of the Puritans of Massachusetts.

* Author's Note: Mrs. Hutchinson was probably a victim of Gov. William Kieft's War, 1643-1645, in which Indians retaliated for the Dutch attacks on Pavonia (NJ) and Corlears Hook (NY).

Herbal Medicines

I had been studying Indian medicines, so when I came back from "captivity" I was a ready-made "medicine man." Put that together with my practice as a chirurgion, and I had a good source of income on Long Island. People would gladly pay me two cows to cure them of their ills. Here is a catalogue of Indians' healing herbs that I have compiled, along with their effects.

Alder bark. Chewed and put on a skinned knee.

Board pine. It is a very large tree, yielding a turpentine.
    The Indians use the moss, boiled in spring water,
        stamping it between stones and applied to stab wounds.

Dogstones, a kind of satyrion. A woman once compounded
    the solid roots of this plant with wine, concocting a love potion.

Green spruce. The tops of the boughs boiled in beer and
    drunk is one of the best cures for scurvy.

Hemlock. The bark is broken, smashed betwixt two stones,
    and made into a plaster. It will heal a sore or swelling.

Indian physic. For preventing fevers.

Milk-weed. For pleurisy.

Oak of Cappadocia. Excellent for stuffing the lungs upon colds.

Primrose. I healed an Indian, whose thumb was swollen,
    extending to his wrist, by mixing *Umbellicus veneris*
        root with egg yolk, and wheat flower.

Robert plantin. A valuable antidote, a.k.a. "Snake Root."

Squasweed. For rheumatism.

Sumach. Boil it in beer and drink it for colds.

Tobacco. Boiled in water, put on a burn or scald, then strewn
    on dried Tobacco powder.

Wood-bine. Good for swellings of the legs.

The most common diseases in New England are the Black Pox, the Spotted Fever, the Griping of the Guts, the Dropsie, and the Sciatica.

How I Met My Wife

One day, I was freshly returned from a trip, riding hither and yon to do deeds of help and healing, and working such marvels as were possible with the few instruments I could carry, supplemented by tar, which I burned from the native pines, and the medicinal herbs that I raised in my little garden. That morning I sat quietly eating my breakfast when there came a knock on the door. I went to the door, there to be met by a man from the neighboring tobacco plantations, saying that he wished me to accompany him to an inn. His daughter had met with an accident, as he said, her horse had thrown her as she was returning from a visitation, and while she had been able to remount and ride to that inn, the darkness and storm had persuaded her to spend the night there. He asked if I could go to her assistance.

The man's name was John Alberti, who lived nearby in Moopit Kills. As it was my sworn duty to help the sick, to her assistance I happily went. Her name was Isabel. I took care of her, we liked each other very much, and as soon as she was sufficiently recovered, we were married. We named our children **Samuel** ('88), David ('92), Elizabeth ('96), William ('98), Mary ('99), Hannah ('00) and John ('09).

We made many moves after that, first to Jamaica, in Queens, where Isabel's brothers lived. My practice flourished there, and I became quite wealthy. Then we moved to Shrewsbury, New Jersey, south of New York City. Finally, we decided to go down south to de la Ware, where I was able to accumulate 200 acres in Wolf Pit Neck. There was a Presbyterian congregation in Lewes, who were much more friendly to the Scots than were the Indians of Long Island or New Jersey.

3

Samuel Stewart
1688-1768

About 80 miles south of Lewes, off the Delaware Peninsula, there is an island called Chincoteague. On this island wild horses roam freely. In my youth, I took the liberty to rustle a few mares and a sire from among them. They are fine steeds, though rather smaller than other horses. The locals call them Chincoteague ponies. Having acquired a small herd of horses, and many cattle, we were starting to outgrow our land in Delaware, so at fifty-three years of age I took my leave of my father and relocated to Augusta, Virginia, in the Shenandoah Valley.

In those days many of the settlers constantly moved up and down the coast, or east and west in the colonies, buying and selling land. Our neighbors in Lewes were the Harrisons. They and several other families went with us to Virginia. In fact, I married their daughter Elizabeth (we called her Lydia to distinguish her from her mother, whose name was the same). Our children were Samuel Jr. ('27), David ('32), John J. ('35), Benjamin ('36), Isaiah ('38), **Joseph** ('40), and John ('44, who married Daniel Boone's sister Hannah). We lived there happily, but not quite "ever after."

In 1753 I received a warrant for five hundred acres in North Carolina from the Earl of Granville, who was hoping to populate his colony with families. Our two oldest sons had already removed there with Lydia's father, so we took our remaining five children and moved to Rowan County. I was sixty-five years old at the time.

The Great Wagon Road

The chill, biting winds of early winter were gone. Now was the balmy breath of early spring. Our friends bade us fare-thee-well; they would continue their lives in Virginia. Now we were going to an unknown home in an unknown land, among unknown neighbors.

It was called the Great Wagon Road, but you would hardly call it "great" from the looks of it. It was more like a muddy rut, all covered with manure from hogs being herded north to market. We set out from Staunton and forded the Folly Mills Creek. It was mostly up hill and down, and we constantly had to push the wagon, or hold it back by ropes that we fastened to the rear. Once we had to take off half our load in order to climb a hill, for it was so slippery the horses could not keep their footing but fell constantly to their knees. Then we came to Lexington. At Natural Bridge, we crossed Cedar Creek, and then took the ferry at Buchanan. In Amsterdam we stopped at the house of Mr. Joseph McDonald.

Tales of the Old Country

Mr. McDonald had recently returned from a trip and told us many a tale about the Old Country. He told us how Alan Breck Stewart, of the Appin Clan, shot Colin Campbell, "The Red Fox," in Lettermore Wood. Alan fled to France, so the Campbells caught James Stewart of the Glen and accused him of participating in the crime "in art and in part." A jury made up entirely of Campbells found James guilty and hanged him.

"Typical Campbell treachery," I muttered, wondering at how things had deteriorated. My own great-grandmother was a Campbell.

Mr. McDonald also told us that Britain had erased the dates September 3rd through 13th from the calendar, changing the dates from the Julian Calendar to the Gregorian Calendar.

"They did that in Italy in 1583," I commented.

"What about little Nancy?" Lizzy chimed in, referring to our imaginary "granddaughter." This was a family joke about our youngest son Joseph having a baby last year when he was twelve. "She was 'born' on September 13th."

"I guess she wasn't 'born' then," I quipped, "so she won't be having a birthday party this year."

We all had a good laugh over "Nancy." Then we had a good cry over James of the Glen. Finally, we had a good shot of Scotch whiskey, and a good night's sleep. In the morning, we said our good-byes.*

Trouble-makers

In Roanoke County we passed the Black Horse Tavern but didn't stop. We had drunk enough whiskey the night before. We took the upper road among the foothills, with all that involved of toil and struggle, as our *over*-loaded wagon was pushed and pulled up steep hills, rough with stones, slippery with mud, slick with ice, or as it plunged to apparently certain destruction down some precipitous descent where locked wheels and a drag seemed scarcely to check the speed. Now we were taking the lower road, bad in many places it is true, but far easier to travel.

We were dependent on such advance information as we could gain from passing travelers, but at the mercy of any who for love of mischief, or pure meanness, might lead us into difficulties – as had happened on one never-to-be-forgotten night of storm (when we were led on a path to nowhere). Every spring, every stream, every possible camping place was new to us; every fork in the road, every ford, every ferry.

* Author's Note: This episode fictionalizes certain inconsistencies found on Internet sites (there are many), specifically, that a child named Nancy was born in 1752 to Joseph, who was born in 1740, and his wife Sarah [sic], who was born in 1743.

We left Roanoke and forded the river, coming at length to Maggoty Gap. After camping for a spell in Henry, Virginia, we came to a beautiful lowlands with many grapes. Soon we forded the Smith River, and experiencing better weather, we went on to Blackberry Creek, where a man named John Hickey ran a store. This was the last place to buy salt until we could reach our destination. Shortly thereafter it began to rain, so we camped in Horse Pasture until the weather improved.

How We Measured the Distance

At last we came to the North Carolina State Line. We had so far traveled 180 miles from our shove-off point in Augusta. The usual method of counting miles was to tie a rag to a spoke on the wagon wheel and count the revolutions, then multiply by the wheel's circumference (6,000 revolutions equal 15 miles; twelve times fifteen equal 180 miles). The trouble with this method is that your rag gets mighty twisted up. No, instead of doing this, I rigged up a dowel pin on the back wheel, and this would trigger a little bell each time the wheel turned. Our youngest boy Joseph was at the age when boys become contrary, and in need of a task by which to pass the time on our journey. Rather than asking him to count pinecones, I assigned him the task of tallying the rings of that bell (by State Line, 72,000 rings were getting on everyone's nerves).

At Sandy Ridge we left the trail to descend to the creeks to fetch some water. Clouds began to gather in the early morning, and about noon they came together to give us terrible lightning and thunder. Torrents of rain poured down such as we never saw before; there was probably a cloudburst somewhere near. The wind came from all parts of heaven, but chiefly from the northwest and with great force. In a short time the streams rose and came over their banks. All meadows, roads, and many fields were under water. Many fences and bridges were carried away, and when the rain finally stopped toward evening it left a scene of desolation.

We crossed the Meho River and entered North Carolina. At Dodgetown we turned southwest over Bumpy Hollow Road. The next day we reached the Dan River, but it was swollen from recent heavy rains, and we waited for two days. Finally we crossed the Dan and camped there at Walnut Cove. Our sons went ahead with axes and grubbing hoes to clear the road and cut down trees on the steep banks of the creeks. At last we reached the boundary of our tract, which was on the Yadkin River.

The entire trip took a month. It had taken David and Grandpa Harrison over three months, because they had to clear the trails as they went.

Die Wachau

A colony of Germans lived near the Yadkin River. They came down from Pennsylvania about the same time that we came. They had received a hundred thousand acres from Earl Granville, and now they were building a town which they called Salem.

These Germans were devout Christians: I think they were Lutherans. They had what they called "Love-feasts," and organized their society into "choirs," that is, a Married Choir, a Single Choir, a Boys Choir, a Choir of Single Sisters, a Choir of Girls, and a Little Choir of Widows. I heard that later they had a Little Choir of Negroes, when they had enough money, and a Little Choir of Cherokees, but the government forced them to quit that last activity. When these choirs sang together, in the company of trumpets and trombones, it was a marvel to behold. But they weren't Presbyterians.

4

Joseph G. Stewart
1740-1823

It was in the same year that King George III took the crown, I think, that the Creeks and Cherokees declared war on all white men. There was great alarm on the Yadkin, and the country was much disturbed – a large party of Indians was coming our way. In February, they attacked Fort Dobbs.

Sometime about a month later, a young girl came frantically to our house on horseback, screaming that Indians were swarming all over her house. I told her to stay with my mother and rode that way. Along the way I met Mr. William Fish, the girl's father, who had gone with her brother to get provisions. A party of Indians shot a great many arrows at us, killing both Mr. Fish and his son. One arrow pierced me through and through, and another lodged in my shoulder blade. For my soul's sake I rode into the river to escape the savages, only to find more Indians on the far side, but they paid no attention to me. I re-crossed the river and plunged into the woods, where in the darkness and rain I soon lost my way. Wounded by two arrows I wandered for many hours but finally reached a town where a doctor took out the arrows and saved my life.

The next night there arose a strong wind, and on it came the sound as of the howling of a hundred wolves. On that night a snow fell, which stopped the activities of the Indians for a few days; otherwise, the danger continued. Soon news came that John Thomas, a Baptist minister, had been killed nearby. The Indians burned houses on the Yadkin River, which was where my brother David lived. Two people were killed on the Town Fork, and there were Indian spies every night. The Indians presented a danger for many years after that, but with the increased presence of our militia, life could be lived in a somewhat normal manner.

I Get Married (1)

When I was 28 years of age, I married Mary Tucker. We lived on a small part of my father's land and had four children: Margaret ('69), Joseph ('70), Benjamin ('72), and John ('74). Sadly, my wife Mary died when little John was born.

The Great Awakening

I was raised a Presbyterian, but there were no other Presbyterian congregations near where we lived in North Carolina. One day I went with my brothers John and Benjamin down to a town called Sandy Creek, where there was going to be a revival meeting. The preacher there, a Mr. Stearns, had left his Congregational church in Virginia after hearing George Whitefield preach in

Boston. We were surprised by the number of people who were there – about six hundred in all. He had a booming voice, but that wasn't the half of it. There was fire in his speech. They were "New Light" Baptists.

The Old Light Baptists were more moderate. They didn't like to have revivals. The New Lights were dynamic and evangelical. They strictly adhered to John Calvin's doctrine of predestination, and they practiced nine rituals – baptism by full immersion, foot washing, taking the Lord's Supper, the laying on of hands, the right hand of fellowship, the kiss of charity, anointing the sick, having love feasts, and devotion to children. Anyone called by the Holy Spirit could preach in their church. They condemned public dancing, gambling, and breaking the Sabbath. At the end of the day, my brothers and I had become New Light Baptists.

I Get Married (2)

In 1775, at thirty-five years of age, I married Sarah Gilbert, whom we called "Morgan." We had more children: **Samuel P.** ('81), David ('84), William ('88), and Jesse ('90).

Just after our wedding, a black and red spider bit me on the lip as I was putting my horse into a stall. My lip soon swelled, and for many hours I lay speechless and unconscious, and nearly died. They say the color of my face resembled that of the spider. Sarah sent for the German doctor, who was called Brother Hans Kalberlahn. He applied the juice of *Robert Planting* (Snake Root), the herb for poisons, which healed me.

The Course of Human Events

I was thirty-six years old when the Revolution broke out. Though I tried to volunteer for Patriot service they rejected me, because I had been shot with those Indian arrows. To prove I could still function normally, I invited the recruiting officer to go with me a little way out into the woods. Then I made a wager with him. If I could cut down a tree in such a way that it fell in precisely the spot that I pointed out beforehand, he would let me join the army... as an officer. If not, I would go home to my family, and leave the war to him and his recruits. I chose the spot (a tree stump) and proceeded to cut down a spruce tree with my axe. The officer was so impressed that I was able to place that falling tree with such precision that he assigned me to the North Carolina 9th Regiment, under the leadership of Colonel John P. Williams. I held the rank of Lieutenant.

After the war was over, I took our family over the big, blue mountains. We went to Overton County, Tennessee, where we joined the Roaring River Baptist Church.

5

Samuel P. Stewart

1781-1824

When I was 18 years old, I moved to Tennessee with my father and mother. Leaving from the head of the Yadkin River, we traveled westward, heading up for Moccasin Gap in the Clinch Mountains, crossing the Blue Ridge to the three forks of New River, then over Stone Mountain. Next, we went over Iron Mountain into the Holston River Valley until we arrived on a stream south of Long Island, there to live in the Washington District of North Carolina.

The next year, I was lucky enough to marry Mary Polly Kitchner. We had eight children: Sarah Sallie ('02), David ('04), Christopher Columbus ('06), Benjamin Kendrick ('08), John Gilbert ('11), **David Kimbrough** ('13)*, Samuel B ('15) and Joseph P ('18).

Later we moved from Washington County down around to Livingston, Tennessee, East of Nashville.

I Till the Soil

Let me tell you the life of a farmer, namely, me. These are pages from my diary, so they follow along season by season.

In March we measured out the orchard, planting apple and peach trees. We had to buy seedlings in town. We went to get corn for the horses that will help us plough the fields. We cleared land for a corn field (we can clear four acres in a week). It rained a lot, which was good for our garden. The air dries the ground quickly here, and there is generally a good deal of wind.

In April we planted corn, with pumpkins and beans in between the rows. We went to town and got four bushels of seed potatoes and planted them. It was very cold, and blossoms and young plants were somewhat hurt. We burned brush, cleared the field, and planted hemp seed.

In May we began to fence in an eight-acre cow pen. We split rails for a seven-rail fence. We planted cotton seed and hauled oak bark for the tannery. We girdled trees, we felled and split some more trees. We weeded our garden and fields and began to hoe corn which was planted in April.

In June we began to plant more corn. We split more rails. Then we separated the calves from the cows, and herded cows in the forest. We made a cow pen, aside of the calf pen. Then we made a feeding trough from a tree. We began to pull flax and began the haymaking. The weather was hot and dry.

* See note, #6 below.

In July we picked the ripe barley from among the oats and began to cut wheat. We guarded our millet from the birds and watched for three weeks until the millet was cut and threshed. Then we gathered blackberries for vinegar, stacked our grain and began to plough the fields from which grain was gathered.

By August we had planted buckwheat. We made a threshing floor and completed the churn. Then we cut logs for corn cribs. We looked in the woods for cattle which had strayed and found them. Then we cut fodder and gathered the hemp. In August, the second hay harvest began. In the latter days there was much rain, which interfered with the haymaking.

We now have 12 cows and 12 calves, one bull and one steer. The cattle are very wild, we feed them little and let them run in the woods. At night we tie them to their feed troughs.

Our usual and best food is milk and mush, and whatever can be made from cornmeal. We shoot a few deer and small bears. That is all the meat we have. Game is scarce, so we do little hunting.

Our garden has served us well: from May to July we had salad every day for dinner, and nearly every evening also. When the salad came to an end, we had cucumbers for three weeks, with three or four meals of sugar peas, beans, occasionally cabbage, and squashes. Everything grows rapidly here.

A 'Louisiana Purchase'

One day we went over to a mill on the Hiwassee River to barter for some firewood. There was a Frenchman there, an Acadian, just come up from Louisiana. He said he wanted to buy a "stere" of firewood, but the woodcutter insisted that a "steer" was a bull that had been... well, you know. If he wanted to buy firewood, he would have to buy a "cord." That's four feet by four feet by eight feet, tied with a twenty-four-foot long cord. The Frenchman said that a "stere" was equal to one meter by one meter by one meter. Well now, that caused quite a ruckus.

"I do know a bit about poetry," the woodcutter replied. "One type of meter is I-am-bick."

"Nuh say pah, noh!" countered the Frenchman.

"Another is an-a-pest-ick."

"Sacre bleu!" exclaimed the Frog. He said they had fought a revolution in France over just such a thing.

"I also know about duck-tillick." said the woodsman.

"Firewood," I chimed in. "Let's get on with it. How long do I have to wait for a cord of firewood?"

"You'll have to wait for this gentleman," the woodsman replied. "He got here before you."

What ensued was a heated argument over the relative value of different systems of measurement. The woodsman, a man of old English stock, was adamant: Queen Elizabeth proclaimed it, so that made it true: a chain was 22 yards long, a furlong was ten chains, and a mile was eight furlongs.

"Kahrant!" exclaimed the Frenchman, adding twenty-two plus ten plus eight to give him the French equivalent of "forty." Then he embarked on a tirade about the merits of his so-called "meters," which he claimed were God-given units equaling one ten-millionth of the arc of the earth.

"A *hectare* is a hundred *ares*," continued the Frenchman. "That's enough land to support your entire family for a week."

"Must be about four acres," I mused, growing more and more impatient. "If you don't shut up, I'll take it out of your *hide*." I was referring to the English unit of 120 acres, enough to support an entire family for a year. "Then I'll *steer* one cubic 'meter' of firewood right up your *arse!*"

I call that episode "A Louisiana Purchase," because that Frenchman came from Louisiana. The real "Louisiana Purchase" was the one that President Jefferson made. I guess France needed some money to pay for their Revolution, so we bought a huge amount of land from them on the other side of the Ol' Mississip'.

How I Died

One day while I was plowing, I was "bustin' middle" – riding a Lister "middle-buster" with a four-horse team – when suddenly, for one reason or another, the team bolted. As they bolted forward the neck yoke broke and the tip of the tongue dropped, plowing into the ground. With the horses bolting forward and the tongue tip dug deep into the ground and the horses still pulling on the traces, the force was too much on the tongue and it broke with a snap near my driver's seat. Busted in the middle. Still holding the reins, I was being pulled forward with such momentum that the immoveable stationary object – the wagon tongue – drove the jagged end of the hardwood tongue up through one of my legs and right up through the pelvic area. Somehow Polly got me up to the house and summoned a doctor, but he said there was nothing he could do to save my life.

Polly sat with me day and night during my last few days on earth. That last afternoon she said she was going to rest for a while, when I looked up at her and said, "Be sure to be back before nine o'clock for I won't be here after then."

Our children were still very young, though Sarah Sallie had just married a good man. Christopher Columbus was eighteen, so he would not pose any problem, but our youngest, Joseph, was only six. Polly would have her hands full taking care of those children all by herself.

6

Rev. David Kimbrough Stewart

1813-1878

A picture is worth a thousand words:

D.K. Stewart and his wife Margaret Alice (née Robertson)

* Author's Note: There is some controversy as to whether David Kimbrough Stewart is the son of Samuel P. Stewart and Polly Kitchner, as noted herein, or of Joseph Stewart Jr. and his wife Sarah Copeland. For the purposes of this study, it really doesn't matter, unless you are interested in his maternal ancestry. He is still the grandson of Joseph Sr.

I am in the possession of a family Bible purchased by D.K. Stewart in 1865. He records his and his wife's birthdates but makes no mention of his parents. I would suppose that since Samuel P. died when David was only ten years old, and Polly did not remarry, that the younger children were taken in by their uncle Joseph Jr., a fact which could lead to confusion.

The middle name Kimbrough makes it easy to conduct Internet searches but leaves us with other questions. Middle names often refer to family lines, often on the mother's side, as in the case of John Fitzgerald Kennedy or Richard Milhous Nixon. In other cases, they refer to persons admired by one's parents, as in the case of George Washington Carver, or Martin Luther King. The Kimbroughs were a family of renowned Baptist preachers living in North Carolina at the time. It is possible that David was named after these people, just as his son could have been named after John Thomas, a prominent preacher of the time (see #7 below).

7
John Thomas Stewart
1854-1937

I'm NOT the one they called "Wild John." That was Wild John Davis. He lived in Voca... but he wasn't me. Come to think of it, I was a bit wild, too.

My dad was a minister in the Church of Christ, but he changed to Christadelphian, a new denomination. I think that is why he named me after John Thomas, who was a popular writer back in my father's day and age. Reverend Thomas started the Christadelphian movement.

For years, our family had been staunch believers in the Presbyterian religion. That had all changed when my great-grandfather moved to Carolina, where they became Baptists. I'll never know why my dad became a Church of Christ minister. It could've been that he just liked singing in the church service, which the Presbyterians didn't like doing.

We Christadelphians don't do a lot of singing, but we sure like to worship the Lord! Not only that, but we don't have ministers, like my father. We're all brothers. If anyone wants to lead the service, may the power of the Lord be with him! Next Sunday, it'll be the next man's turn.

Fishers of Men

When I was a boy, my father gave me lessons in "Scriptural geometry." One of the lessons was about a fishing trip, narrated in the last chapter of the Gospel of St. John, when Peter and some other disciples pulled in one hundred fifty-three fish. Why were there exactly one hundred fifty-three fish? Because the boat was 200 cubits away from the shore.

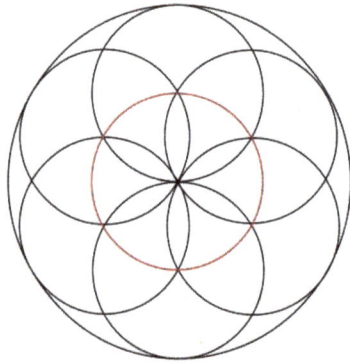

Peter (in red) goes fishing with some other disciples.

In this story Peter and six other disciples go on a fishing trip in the Sea of Tiberias. They get "skunked" while fishing all night, but when morning comes, Jesus tells them to throw their net on the right side of the ship. They do as he says and catch a net full of fish, but they can't haul so many fish to shore!

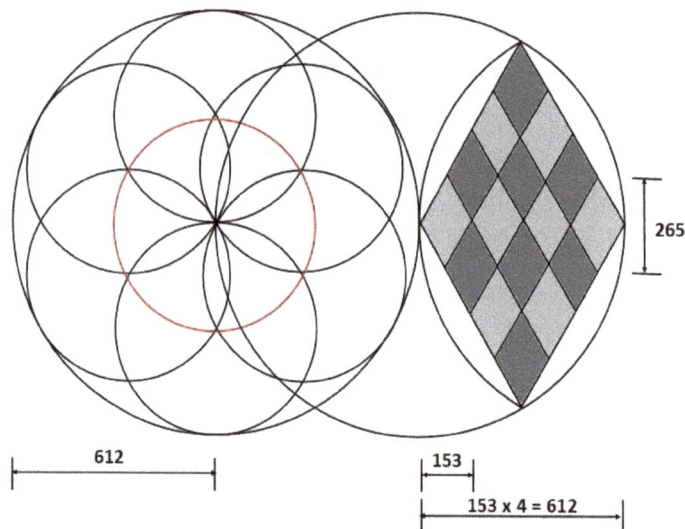

The fishermen catch fish on the right side of the boat.

Peter puts on his raincoat and jumps out of the ship. It is only 200 cubits* from the shore, shallow enough that he can walk, and therefore pull the boat with a rope.

* Author's Note: They are using Greek cubits:

Egyptian Cubit		Greek Cubit		Roman Cubit
1.728 ft	25:22	1.521 ft	25:24	1.459 ft

There is magic in the Greek language. Some people a long time ago assigned a number to each letter of its alphabet, and in this way they could assign a number to names or phrases. They called this "Aesopsifying a word." For example, *Athena* (69) + *Hephaistos* (795) = 864, a magic number.*

In this way the Greek word for *fishes* = 1224. *The net* also equals 1224. The number for *Simon the Peter* is 1925, and *The Good Shepherd* is 612. *Raincoat* is 1060.

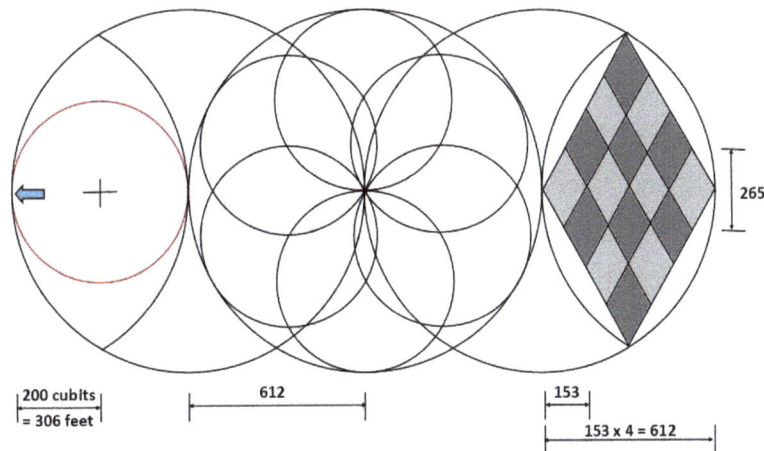

Peter jumps ship and helps pull the boat and net to shore.

If the boat has a diameter of 1224, each disciple's diameter is 612. Therefore, Peter's circumference is 1925. The big rhombus is 612 wide and 1060 high, making each small rhombus 153 wide and 265 high. One Greek cubit equals 1.53 feet, so 200 cubits equal 306 feet, or half of Peter's diameter (612). The raincoat is as tall as the big rhombus.

The number 153 is a magic number. The number 17 (the number of small rhombuses plus the big one) is also a magic number. Lookie here:

$$1+2+3+4+5+6+7+8+9+10+11+12+13+14+15+16+17=153.$$

$$1^3 + 5^3 + 3^3 = 153.$$

$$1! + 2! + 3! + 4! + 5! = 153.$$

* Author's Note: There are 86,400 seconds in a day. There are 86,400,000 Greek cubits in a Great Circle, that is, the circumference of the earth measured through the poles. The diameter of the sun is 864,000 miles. 864/275 = pi.

That old Greek guy, Archimedes, called 153 "the measure of the fish," or the dimensions of the semicircular shape that encloses the "net" in this story. The ratio of the sides of the rhombus (265/153) is the same as that of the Egyptian cubit to the foot. It is also the square root of three.

That's a lot of cubits, eh? I think 153 is just the number of souls a man must save before he can retire from preaching. I am not a preacher, but like the 17-year cicada, I "lay low" for a long time before I finally came out of my shell and got married. (In reality, it took a bit longer than seventeen years.)

In 1877 I married Louisa Ophelia McMillan – best thing I ever did. We had seven children: Cora Lee ('77), David Abney ('79), Charles Madison ('81), Harvey Hugh ('84), Margaret Elsie ('86), **Alva Clinton** ('89), and Atlee Draper ('92).

After Ophelia died (1895), it fell upon my oldest daughter Cora Lee to take care of the children. After the boys were big enough to take care of themselves, I married Virginia "Miss Jenny" Covington and moved out to a town called Staff, near Eastland TX. Miss Jenny was a spinster, fifty years old at the time. She had been a schoolteacher in her younger days – small of frame, very intelligent… and feisty. She had a very solemn countenance about her, and her nose had somewhat of a hawkish appearance. Her eyes tended to be a little "buggy," which unfortunately, all added up to give her an appearance of not being overly intelligent. How one's looks can be so deceiving! She was a sweet, kind, affable soul, a tiny woman but with great inner strength. She always addressed me as "Mr. Stewart."

Ophelia McMillan　　　　John and "Miss Jenny"　　　　John in his Old Age

When we (rather, *I*) decided to leave Texas and move out to California to live in Alvie's little place on Myrtle Street (in Pomona), Miss Jennie was thoroughly opposed. She was completely attached to Texas. All her friends and possessions were there. When asked why she didn't want to go she said, "I don't want to leave all my little pots and pans," for these were all her worldly treasures.

8

Alva Clinton Stewart

1889-1956

I was born March 19, 1889 in Burnet, Texas. My mom died when I was six, so my sister Cora Lee pretty much raised us kids. I was the second youngest of seven kids, so I was down near the bottom of the "pecking order," so to speak.

One of my first jobs was selling Watkins Liniment door-to-door. I had to wear a white suit (the good guys always wear white, you know) and walk around with my case of samples. It was a pretty good deal. Each bottle had a "trial mark" on it, which meant that you could use the liniment down to that mark, and if you didn't like it, you could get your money back. Not too many people requested a refund. A few did.

As luck would have it, I went selling potions at the Christadelphian Church Campground in Stonewall (it was actually closer to Hye, on the east side of the L.B.J. ranch). Minnie Passmore and her sister Leah were sitting on the stoop. As they say, I chased Minnie until she caught me.

Minnie and I tied the knot in 1913. There were a lot of German immigrants in Texas in those days, so we had a Lutheran wedding.* All of Minnie's relatives hopped onto their wagons and buggies and came down from Brady to attend. Now the minister, being Lutheran, didn't believe the service was valid if spoken in English, so when he was finished, he started up all over again, this time speaking German! Needless to say, it was a long wedding ceremony.

* Author's Note: There was a conscious effort, beginning in 1842, to promote German colonization in Texas. Count Victor August and Count Carl of Castell, with the help of Prince Frederick of Prussia, purchased an interest in the Fisher-Miller Land Grant. Prince Solms and Baron Meusebach played an active role in populating the area and, once Texas became a state (1846), negotiated a peace with the local branch of Comanche Indians.

It was ironic that old Mr. Schreiner, who had been a captain in the Texas Rangers, served as a private in the Confederate Army. We still called him "Captain," though. After the war he made a ton of money driving longhorns up through Comanche territory to Dodge City. Some cattlemen were not able to negotiate passage with the Indians, but I think Capt. Schreiner persuaded them with a bit of old-fashioned moxie, more than just a few pounds of (longhorn) flesh, and a generous supply of whiskey. That's how he got rich. At the apex of his career, he had amassed about 600,000 acres of land. Then he started a department store, and he even put a bank inside it.

I worked as a ranch hand. That meant doing just about anything they asked you to do, but I figured that up to that point the only two things I had ever done were shoveling bat guano in Carlsbad Caverns and selling some smelly rubbing oil. Anyway, the pay was better, so I would do it.

Shortly after little Jack was born, Capt. Schreiner decided to divvy up his holdings among his eight children. The ranch at Junction, where I worked, went to one of his daughters. She didn't want to continue the ranching business, so she sold the property off to various bidders. I was out of work.

Pomona

My big brother Harvey had gone out to California, where he worked in a walnut grove near Pomona, east of Los Angeles. He heard I had lost my job and told me I would be much better off if I joined him out west. It sounded nice, but I didn't have enough money to relocate my family to such a distant place.

We had an older brother, Abney, who said I could probably get a job working for the railroad, which I did. I worked there long enough to save up money for the trip. When the time came, we headed out to California.

That was not an easy trip in a Model T Ford. You had to venture out through the Badlands of New Mexico first. That is such an eerie sight – you almost expect dinosaurs to come out from behind those red bluffs at any time. Next you go through Arizona, which can be beautiful, in a desert sort of way. After that you come to the real desert, the Mojave. The road there is just a bunch of railroad ties laid together; they can be moved to adjust to the shifting sands. Then you come to a town called Barstow, which is not much more than a gas station and a general store - not the kind of place anyone would want to call home.

Finally, there was Pomona. Harvey was right. It was lush and green, a seeming paradise, after traversing that desert. We settled into a little house on Myrtle Street, and I found work (again) for the railroad.

We bounced around quite a bit in those days, living in railroad owned houses, which were always painted with a queer yellow color. Then I got a job as a horticulturalist, working for the Kellogg Ranch, which raised Arabian horses. My little grandson [yours truly] never knew, when he went there for some peace and quiet on rainy days, that I was the one who had planted those gardens, amid the wet bamboo.

Alvie and Minnie

Alvie and Diane

Union Oil, Brea

I finally took a job as a roughneck, working for Union Oil in Brea. I was lucky, because when the Great Depression struck in 1929, a lot of people lost their jobs. Union Oil was more benevolent. Though our workload was reduced to 3 1/2 days per week (4 days one week, 3 days the next), nobody was laid off entirely.

I put in 25 years with the Union Oil Company, but when they started to unionize (ironic word, isn't it?), the older employees stood a chance of losing our provident fund savings, which was our company retirement fund, so I resigned. I got a job with a small oil company, but I fell off the "doghouse" (the belt and engine housing for those "grasshopper" oil pumps – see illustration on page 33) and injured my kidney, so I had to quit for good.

We bought 300 acres south of Voca, Texas, near where Minnie's sister Leah and her husband lived. Having experience in drilling, I went into the irrigation business, drilling water wells.

One fine January day I went out to work on expanding a water well with Minnie's younger brother Daymon. We had almost finished our morning's labors, but Daymon said he had to drop one more charge before taking a lunch break. My tummy was rumbling, but I guessed I could wait a while. Minnie said she would fix up some fried chicken for…

9
Leonard Jackson Stewart
1914-1988

Childhood

I was born in Junction, Texas, in 1914, the oldest of three boys. We moved around a lot when I was a kid, and that is probably the main reason why, when I was older, I bought a lot and built a house, in which to settle down with my family.

My dad had a lot of different jobs, so we moved back and forth between Texas and Pomona, California (where my brothers were born). Finally, we settled in Brea, where Dad got a job with the Union Oil Company.

High School

I must say, and I firmly believe, that my high school days were the high point of my life. I was in the band, I played sports, and I was a cheerleader. Can you believe it? I did all three!

As for music, I played the violin, at first. Then my parents scrounged up enough to buy me a saxophone, and I was in seventh heaven! Eventually I took up the clarinet, which I considered my main instrument. As for sports, I did everything, but my forté was football: I was the quarterback. When I had time, I would sideline myself and lead the crowd in cheers.

Doggonit! I graduated from Brea-Olinda High School in 1933.

Odd Jobs

After the Crash of '29, jobs were hard to come by, so when I got out of high school, I had to take whatever I could get... picking tomatoes, hoeing weeds, carrying hod, etc. I was a good saxophone player, and gigs were plentiful (and *much* more enjoyable), so I did a lot of night work. One memorable gig came after I was fired from my hod carrying job. Some fellows that I knew

29

came up my front walk and said that one of their members had found a permanent job at SoCal Edison, so could I join them up in Big Bear, playing at the Peter Pan Club? I accepted, of course. It was a private club for movie stars, the pay was good, and it offered steady work through the summer.

Angel on My Couch

While I was away at San Jose State College, my parents moved to a house at 303 S. Brea Boulevard, in Brea. One year I came home for the summer and lolled about, not even bothering to shave for several days at a time. Then one afternoon I came home and found… an Angel on my Couch! She was a friend of my cousin Wanna*, and she had come out from Montebello to see her. Wanna wasn't home at the moment, so she just came in and sat down to wait. This Angel had a name – Faye Milor. "I am pleased to make your acquaintance," I told her. "May I see you again?" "We'll see," she replied, with pun fully intended.

And see her I did. Again and again and again. I had gone to Texas with my parents immediately after that first blissful encounter, but when I got back, I made sure to call that Angel called Faye before I went back to college in San Jose. From then on, every break, every vacation, every chance I had, I would take her out on a date.*

The Big Band Theory

While I was growing up, most social dances were waltzes and polkas. After the "Roaring Twenties," people started doing swing dances, like the foxtrot (a kind of waltz in 4-4 time) or the jitterbug. These were accompanied by big bands which played written compositions and smooth arrangements, instead of improvising like most of the earlier jazz bands did.

Big bands usually had four sections: trumpets, trombones, saxophones, and a rhythm section. When one section would do a sectional "solo," all its members would stand up. Some bands dropped the jazz clarinet, but Artie Shaw and Benny Goodman (my idols) were two band leaders who kept these, mainly because *they* played the clarinet!

Some other big bands featured instrumentalists, such as the trombone of Jack Teagarden, the trumpet of Harry James, the drums of Gene Krupa, and the vibraphone of Lionel Hampton.

* Author's Note: This episode is parodied in *Collected Short Stories*, by E.J. Stewart.

In those days, we danced the Balboa. This swing dance took its name (obviously) from the Balboa Pavilion on Balboa Island in Newport Beach, where we danced to the music of Jimmy Dorsey's Orchestra. The dance was like the Lindy Hop or the Jitterbug, but it was designed for small spaces or crowded dance floors. It used an upright body posture, a close embrace, and shuffling footwork. It featured music such as "Melancholy Baby" by Tommy Dorsey (Jimmy's brother), and "Begin the Beguine" by Artie Shaw.

Faye and I tied the knot at the Little Kirk on the Heather in Las Vegas, January 1, 1942. Sadly, our firstborn died in infancy. Happily, we had three more children after that: two girls and a boy.

Jack, Faye, Baby Jan, Diane

Meditating on the Trombone Positions

Pearl Harbor, 1941. Jeannette Rankin should have been horsewhipped. With Faye being pregnant a second time, I thought I could avoid the draft, but I was wrong. Although my job description was "musician," I wound up in General James Bradley's 96th "Deadeye" Division. During basic training in Oregon we were ordered to march before the commanding officers. One of them complained that our trombone section couldn't move their slides in unison. He even reprimanded us in writing. The fool didn't know that they were playing different parts, and trombones are played that way. Under this kind of leadership we went to war in 1944.*

The Secret Code

Before I shipped out, Faye and I had devised a code to let her know where I was going. (We were never told where we were going until we were out to sea: "Loose lips sink ships," as the posters read.) "On the highway" meant *Hawaii*, where I was sent first, before heading into the combat zone. "I'll be late" meant the island of *Leyte*. On Leyte, we were not on the front lines of combat, but we were stationed on the ground, doing such duties as standing guard over a downed,

* Author's Note: L.J.S. gives some details of the war, but he understates the severity of the conflict. Leyte and Okinawa were two of the most gruesome battles in all history. He was lucky to have been in the rearguard.

31

but injured, pilot. During this stint I guided Gen. Douglas MacArthur out to his meeting with our commander, Gen. Bradley. "My cousin from Oklahoma" meant *Okinawa*, as people from that state were called "Okies," and my cousin, Faye's friend, was named Wanna. Finally, we were pulled back to a remote island in the Philippines, in anticipation of being sent to Korea, whence we would invade Japan, but lords Uranium and Plutonium spared us that grief. I wondered how they could have crammed a three-acre nuclear fission device into the space of one tiny bomb?

Those Who Can, Do. Those Who Can't Do, Teach

Woe unto me, after I got out of the service Faye and I took a day trip up to Mt. Baldy (Mt. San Antonio) to play in the snow (the Pacific islands were hot… what a relief to throw a snowball again). But every silver lining has a cloud – I came down with a case of Bell's Palsy after that. Besides not being able to close my left eye, my mouth was too weak to play any kind of reed instrument at all. So ended my career as a bandsman.

From that time on I concentrated on building a career as a public-school music teacher. I spent a summer in Chicago at the VanderCook School of Music, learning what needed to be learned (besides music) for a successful career in the schools, namely, pageantry. In other words, learning to play the instruments or sing was not enough; kids in secondary musical groups were expected to march in parades or present half-time shows at football games. Not only that, but I would have to recruit students if I wanted to keep my job. Below is an example of a poster I prepared for recruitment.

This is what Mr. Stewart teaches in his music classes:

Notes – to you.	Clef – what people fall off of.
Treble – what bad boys get into.	Tuba – tooth paste.
Minor – yours.	Oboes – tramps.
Duet – and you get a whippin'.	Bow* – a date.
Alto – gather.	Cello – six delicious flavors.
Tenor – eleven.	Staff – and nonsense.
Bass – handy in baseball.	Trombones – and dog-biscuits.
Trill – of a lifetime.	

I had a "pipe dream," pun fully intended. My dad and his brothers inherited the mineral rights to some land in Eastland, Texas. When I retired from teaching, I figured I could set my family up financially if I pursued the drilling of an oil well on this land. This was not as easy as I thought. For one thing, the land was now a golf course, and the owner would in no way allow a drilling rig to be set up in the middle of the fairway. We solved that problem by drilling an oblique well, from the side.

The other problem that we encountered was insurmountable. It seems that my cousins owned half of the inherited mineral rights, and for some unexplained reason they absolutely refused to pursue my dreams any further… even after we had struck oil!

Oh, well. To each his own. It wasn't worth a family feud.

Leonard J. Stewart

* "Santa Fe had a <u>beau</u>. His name was Denny Cottontail."
   … from *Collected Short Stories*, by E.J. Stewart

10

Jan E.J. Stewart

1948-

Mine is a tale of two windmills, if you will. Though I was born in Montebello, California (where my grandparents lived), my parents lived in Solvang, which had a windmill. On the east coast, in New Amsterdam, Epke Jacobse had a windmill (he had left his old windmill in Holland). Our home was a little duplex, which is now a Danish Pastry shop.

Solvang

Before I knew it, my parents moved to 2828 Mayflower Street, in Arcadia. At five years of age, I enrolled in Plymouth Elementary School. A real Pilgrim, I was.

One of my earliest memories was being on the Howdy Doody Show. I thought it strange that my father should not take me to Sunday School that day. After all, going to Sunday School was one of the Ten Commandments of childhood. (Can you guess what the other nine were?) Anyway, we drove down into some residential neighborhood in Bellflower, or someplace, and found the "studio." It was not your typical TV studio at all, more like someone's house that doubled as a TV studio.

The Howdy Doody Show made a good metaphor that served me from that day forward. I learned then and there that life is all bright lights and dummies.

Summer Vacations

When I was six years old, we took the airplane to Chicago. It was a propeller plane, a DC-3. From there we rented a car and drove to Detroit. My father had ordered a new car directly from the factory, and we went to pick it up. It seemed to take forever, waiting out there in the rented car between long rows of "Mo-Town" factory buildings. The car finally came out – a 1954 Buick Century, turquoise and white, with its trademark "port-holes" behind the front wheels.

So began one of our yearly summer vacations (a perk of public school teachers, which was my father's job). At the time I didn't really enjoy these trips. I got carsick a lot. I guess I should be thankful. The summer vacations gave me the chance to say that I have been to all the Continental 48 states (plus Hawaii, not by DC-3, thank heavens!).

Good things that stand out in my memory are the endless hills of states like Kentucky, driving up and down, through covered wooden bridges, through miles and miles of trees, finally arriving at a splendid view of the gold-domed state capitol building. All those Colonial states were more or less variations on the same theme.

On these trips we often stopped for lunch at picnic tables alongside the road, or in national parks. I don't remember which park we were visiting, but something very remarkable happened while we were eating our Spam sandwiches. A bear came along and crawled into our 1954 Buick. He got into the driver's side window (luckily my father hadn't left the keys in the car!), but finding no honey to nibble, the bear crawled out the passenger side window. My father got it all on 8 millimeter film, by the way.

One more thing. My father had a bunch of chinchillas that he hoped he could sell one day for a profit (for making fur coats, I assume). On one trip he asked our neighbors in Arcadia to look after them while we were gone, but upon our return they told us the chinchillas had died in a heat wave. They did not show us their corpses. I always suspected they had sold the chinchillas.

I slay the Singing Asp (1)

On another trip, when I was nine or ten, we stopped back by Grammie Stewart's house in Voca. I was walking with my dad out by the "tank" (they had 300 acres on rocky land), when we stepped on a small ledge in the rock path. Little did we know that a rattlesnake was stretched out sleeping under the ledge. Well, the startled snake let us know that we weren't welcome and jumped in one direction, making a lot of noise about it; we got the message and jumped about ten feet in the other direction. I've never been so scared! But we could've won the Olympics.

36

You just didn't leave a snake to lead its peaceful life, so we went back to finish it off. It had twisted itself up in a bush not far away. I had a little .22 rifle, so I shot it twice, but unless you hit a snake in the head it doesn't die. I finally hit it on its thinking cap. We used a knife and cut its rattles off – it was seven years old, one rattle for each year of its wicked life.

We decided we had better get out of there before its wife came along and took out her wrath on our ankles. They travel in pairs, you know.

Vineyard in a Cove

When I was eight, we moved. My parents bought 2/3 of an acre in an orange grove in Covina ("Vineyard in a Cove"), and we built a ranch-style house there. The address was 19805 E. Cypress Avenue.

This was suburbia. My friends and I used to enjoy going over past San Dimas to the Kellogg House, the most untouched part of the east San Gabriel Valley. There was a brook down there, and we would try to catch polliwogs in our little nets.

World War III

There was one event that you probably won't read about in the history books. I was about ten years old at the time, standing in our front yard. I looked up and saw warplanes buzzing overhead from east to west. Hmm, I thought. What is to the east? Edwards AFB was almost due north of us. Maybe they came out of Edwards and turned west. March Air Base was due east, but they didn't have very many planes. What was to the west? Russia!

As I stood there awestruck, the planes kept coming. I watched for a good half hour, and they didn't stop. I finally went inside the house, preparing to "duck and cover," but the end never came. I waited for my mother to tell me we had to go to Eastland Shopping Center, where they had bomb shelters, but she never mentioned it. Walter Cronkite came on the news; no mention was ever made of the droves of jets that flew over Southern California that day.

From our house on Cypress Avenue, it was a five-minute walk to the newly built Charter Oak High School, which I was destined to attend. One day during my Freshman year, I was walking across the quad on my way to the first class when some guy walked up to me and said, "Did you hear about [then-president] Kennedy? He got shot!" Even for a fifteen-year-old kid, that was serious news. I wondered if he was dead or alive? No students were out and about; even the birds had stopped singing! An eerie silence fell over the land. I didn't care much about Kennedy, but the assassination of a sitting president was a monumental event.

Sports

Like many boys of my age, I enjoyed sports. At various times I played baseball, football, basketball, and I ran track.

As a small kid I played little league baseball: I was a pitcher for the Charter Oak Orioles. I guess that was the main difference between me and my father – he was a catcher; I was a pitcher. Looking back, the pinnacle of my dad's life seemed to be his high school days. For me, high school was not fun; I just had growing pains. My best days were spent in university.

I was a bit surprised at my father, who was an amateur B&W photographer (he even had his own darkroom). He took a million pictures of me in my football uniform, and more of me competing in track meets, but not one of me playing baseball. So, I drew a self-portrait:

I finally strike out Robin White
after he fouls off ten pitches

In my youth, I had three Teutonic friends. Each affected me in his own peculiar way. Terry Shaefer was my first Teutonic friend. He was a simpleton but cheerful, and we had a lot of good times together. One time while we were driving in my '55 Chevy, he pulled the Covico steering wheel off (it had not yet been bolted on properly). I'll never forget his stupid guffawing. Can you imagine trying to steer a car by hand, holding on to nothing but a bolt with your bare fingers?

Though he stood about six inches taller than me, it was this same Terry Shaefer whom I had to pair up with at football practice. We lined up, side by side in two lines facing each other. Then the boys in one line would run full speed at those in the other line and tackle them where they stood. Then the roles were reversed. You would think it somewhat fearful, standing there and letting your Teutonic friend run at you laughing, then tackle you, but it hardly hurt at all; we were well padded. What hurt was when I had to tackle him. He weighed a ton, and as he fell, he crushed my forearms under his massive thighs. Ouch!

After our high school's team won the C.I.F. championship (in my Freshman year), I got on the bandwagon and joined the cross-country team (a 1.8 mile race). This meant I had to quit the football team. I remember those cross-country meets at Mt. SAC. They had this humungous hill that you had to run up to finish the race. My lungs would hurt from breathing the smog. I thought that this was no way for a human being to live. Why breathe such stuff? I vowed one day to leave the San Gabriel Valley. I got along with the people all right; it was just the air pollution. I guess I could read the writing on the wall: it would get worse, in more ways than one; it would never get better.

1966

Azusa Pacific

Though my father was raised in the Christadelphian Church, we followed the "Faith of our Mothers," so to speak, possibly because my mother came from a long line of Baptist ministers. We belonged to the First Baptist Church, which probably grew out of the "Old Light," with the "New Light" becoming the Southern Baptists (see Section #4, above).

I had my share of teenaged angst. In general, I didn't know how to deal with the future. To be specific, I realized that I was not talented at making money… nor anything else. I was twenty-one years old, and I needed to get going. The problem was… where? … how? So it was that I sat down and prayed: "God, if you are real, please show me!"

A guy came up to me at Mt. SAC and invited me to a Friday night concert at St. Lucy's High School for Girls, in Azusa. It was sponsored by a prayer group out of Azusa Pacific College. I figured this was God's answer to my prayer. Following that concert, I went to one of their Wednesday night prayer meetings and became a Christian. It was November. I was baptized the next spring in the Pacific Ocean at Devereux Beach, north of Santa Barbara.

From then on, I attended the "Church in the Park," which was a non-denominational affair sponsored by Azusa Pacific, a Wesleyan Methodist college.

When I moved away to Santa Rosa, I hung a picture of Jesus (that the Parrot Lady had drawn) on my wall. The strangest thing was, when I stared at that picture, Christ indwelled it and spoke to me. Though the Lord had taken my "training wheels" off early, through that picture He kept me from falling down. I attended a Congregational church in Santa Rosa.

Though I had attended many different denominations and styles of churches, probably the one that was most akin to my beliefs was the Seventh-Day Adventist Church. I never joined them, however.

University Life

Franz Sanger was another Teutonic friend. I met him at Mt. SAC when I was 19. He had a friend named Ruthie who had gone to Sonoma State College in Santa Rosa. She told me how nice it was, and I decided to go to school there (by the time I arrived, she had transferred to UCSB). Later, after Ruthie graduated, I transferred to UCSB. "You crazy, crazy fool," she chided me, but it was absolutely the right decision in my life.

I took over a room in the Arrellaga House in Santa Barbara from Chuck DeVore, a guy I knew from Pomona. Scratched in the bedside table were the words, "Life is tough when you're a Brigid," put there by Chuck's girlfriend, whom he later married. After a while I moved to Isla Vista, closer to campus.

My third Teutonic friend was Tim Shallenberger, who lived in Isla Vista. He and his friend Jamie had moved there from St. Louis, members of the Reorganized Church of Latter-Day Saints. They swore up and down that they were not Mormons (whom they called Tower Builders), but they believed in the same fabricated documents. Anyway, they gave me two cats, Tweedledee and Tweedledum.

I Slay the Singing Asp (2)

One summer I went with one of my high school friends to Yosemite National Park, which is famous for its waterfalls. We hitched a ride up to the top of Half Dome and spent the night there in our sleeping bags. An astronomer had his telescope set up on top, and he let us watch the moons of Jupiter. It was an unforgettable event!

The next day we walked back down but stopped to rest at Vernal Falls. A sign warned hikers not to try to walk across the lip of the fall, as one young couple had done in days gone by. It was their final mistake. We played it safe (or so we thought) and took a dip in the pool where the water was calm (it is now against the rules to swim in Emerald Pool). As I dove in, I suddenly understood the true meaning of "melted snow." The water was so cold that it numbed my eyes. I swam as fast as I could to a rock in the middle of the pool and sunned myself to warm up. How I dreaded the return trip, but my friend had already gone back! I finally took the plunge and swam as fast as I could to get back to the Silver Apron.

It was on the way back down to the valley that I slew the Singing Asp. It was sunning itself on the trail, so I found a huge rock and crushed its head. The Song of the Singing Asp would no longer shatter the Peace of the Forest. Its Sting would never again grieve the Mothers of Paradise.

Graduation: "Une Jolie Diplôme"

The Vietnam war ended. Anyway, I had gotten Number 299 in the Lottery, a system for deciding who would get drafted, according to the random order in which our birthdays were picked. It was the only lottery I ever won. It was time to graduate.

I always looked back in dismay at the events that surrounded that war. One of the things that troubled me was the way the news reporters, egged on by Woodward and Bernstein, came to regard themselves as the "4th Estate," an unelected "watchdog branch" of government. Arrogant fools.

The second thing that bothered me was also related to the news media. That is the way they spun the outcome, making it look like the U.S. lost the war. The facts say otherwise. The Paris Peace Accords took place in January 1973. After that the U.S. began to withdraw its forces, believing that the North would uphold its signed agreement. They didn't. Saigon fell to the North Vietnamese in April 1975. Yet how can a country lose a war when it has already withdrawn all its soldiers from the battlefield? Go figure.

I guess it was as ex-President Nixon quipped: "We won the war, but we lost the peace."

A Brief Interlude

Upon graduation from UCSB I took my bicycle and went to Europe to "find myself." So many things happened that I can't give details here, but several things are worth noting.

The first was an incident that happened on the road to Beauvoir, a town in Normandy. I had the habit of taking off my shirt to ride in the countryside, but I thought it might be considered rude to ride shirtless through a town, so I stopped my bike and clothed myself. "As I put on my shirt, he came to determine / just whether I was English or German…" These verses I wrote in my notes, *Poems of Incidence and Reflection* (now lost). At any rate, I stopped my bicycle in front of a farmhouse, and the old farmer, who was probably just a young boy during the Nazi occupation of France, asked me my nationality. My parched mouth could not enunciate the French pronunciation of *Americain*, so I said *Anglais* – "English." He went inside his little farmhouse, where he kept an icebox that resembled a fireplace. From this he withdrew a can of cool grapefruit juice and offered it to me. I knew then, and shall never forget, the true meaning of Gratitude: he was in a way repaying those heroic soldiers who had offered their lives to liberate his homeland from the evil of Nazi occupation. His vicarious offering was a can of grapefruit juice.

Another thing that I learned was how to laugh in the face of adversity. I was riding that ten-speed bike over some pretty rough terrain, and sometimes the tire would hit its natural enemy and "poof" – all the air was gone. One time in France, up around Metz, I think, this happened not once, not twice – but twelve times! My greasy thumb could not quite get the wheel off, and I found that I had been cut several times, so I went to the hospital. "*Laisses-moi faire!*" ("Let me do it!") the nurse commanded me, as I recoiled from her alcohol-soaked swab. Outside, menacing Arabs had stolen my tool kit while I was in *Urgences* ("Emergency"). Groan. I took a bus back to the campground where I was staying. A French man in the seat next to me asked about my wheel, which I carried in the aisle. I told him about my "*douzaines catastrophes*," and he just laughed.

The third thing was a concert by a military band in Saint James Park, London. They were playing a nice arrangement of "Moon River." Nice, but not my cup of tea. Then and there I decided that I would not join the Air Force as a band director. I couldn't imagine spending my life in public parks, playing "easy listening" tunes for Sunday Afternoon audiences. After all, hadn't I quit the brass band after my sophomore year at Charter Oak High School? It really *wasn't* my cup of tea.

Tormenting Catgut

Santa Barbara was a nice place to go to school – a laid back, sleepy town, no problems – but you just couldn't get a job there. After I came back from Europe, I returned to Los Angeles, where I got a job in Manufacturer's Bank. Maybe it was the daily commute (26 miles each way in the traffic and the smog), or maybe it was people's attitudes when it came to their money (that sucked), but after six months I had had enough. I quit and enrolled in the Claremont Graduate School, Dept. of Education.

I was one of three Christians in our class of twenty-five. One day we were discussing some education book when the resident atheist said, "I can't stand the overwhelming Christianity of this." We looked at one another in dismay, for there was nothing even remotely "Christian" about the book we were discussing. "If this overwhelms you," I told him, "you should not attempt to read the Bible – you would be devastated."

During this time, I attended Calvary Chapel in Costa Mesa as often as I could. The Sunday services were nice, but once in a while I would go to the "after-glow" following their Saturday night specials. I didn't speak in tongues, so it was a little strange for me.

The first job I got was in the Centralia School District in Buena Park. I was responsible for music education in two schools, one being – you guessed it – Walter Knott Elementary, right across from Knott's Berry Farm. My two-year contract expired, and I needed to find something else. I wasn't too thrilled about listening to the squawking and scratching noise of kids playing beginning instruments for my whole life (trying to wring the truth out of catgut by twisting pegs, as Plato put it), so I took a job at Chapman College, teaching English. Much better.

The Radcliffe Camera

I liked to study. Maybe that's one reason why I stayed in college so long. In addition to the California colleges, I did a brief stint at Worcester College, University of Oxford. There, I studied Anglo-Saxon England under the tutorship of David Hinton. My paper was a comparison of sunspot cycles with events in the *Anglo-Saxon Chronicle.* I have fond memories of doing research in the Radcliffe Camera (a circular library), and of drinking shandy at the White Horse Inn (a pub) after hours.

One of the main purposes (practically speaking) of educational institutions in America is matchmaking. How can one meet a life partner in the workplace? I stayed in school long enough – why then did I never marry, you may ask.

The answer is many-faceted. I wasn't sure of my career. Should I choose the path of Ichabod Crane (a music teacher), which may have its own headless horseman lurking somewhere in the future (my father, as the music teacher, was first to be laid off in times of economic troubles), or that of Rip van Winkle (an English teacher), which may involve a long, sleepy twenty years. As for marriage, on the Great Carrousel of Life, I did not seize that brass ring as I rode by the first time. I would be sure not to miss the Gold Ring, next time around.

The Origin of the Stewarts

Luke 3:27-31 KJV		Mt. 1:6-12 KJV	
33 King David of Judah 1085-1015 BC		33 King David of Judah 1085-1015 BC	
(Nathan's Line)		(Solomon's Line)	
34 Nathan	1075-	34 King Solomon	962-922
35 Mattatha	964-	35 King Roboam	922-915
36 Menna	943-	36 King Abia	915-913
37 Melea	922	37 King Asa	913-873
38 Eliakim	901-	38 King Josaphat	873-849
39 Jonam	880 BC	39 King Joram	849-842
40 Joseph	860 BC	40 King Ozias	
41 Juda	840 BC	41 King Joatham	742-735 BC
42 Simeon	820 BC	42 King Achaz	735-715
43 Levi	800 BC	43 King Ezekias	715-687
44 Matthat	780 BC	44 King Jotham	
45 Jorim	-760	45 King Ahaz	
46 Eliezer	740 BC	46 King Hezekiah	
47 Jose	720-	47 King Manasses	687-642
48 Er	700 BC -	48 King Amon	641-641
49 Elmodam	695 – 659 BC	49 Josias	649-610
50 Cosam	625 -	50 Eliakim	
51 Addi			
52 Melchi	620 BC	< Babylon >	
53 Neri		51 Jechonias	609
54 Salathiel		52 Salathiel	580 BC -
55 Zorobabel		53 Zorobabel	r. 538-520 BC

from Zorobabel…

Mt. 1:13-16 KJV
56 (Lk) or 54 (Mt) Abiud
57 Eliakim
58 Azor
59 Sadoc
60 Achim
61 Eliud ben Achim
62 Eleazar
63 Matthan
64 Jacob
65 Joseph 44 BC-23 AD
(Husband of Mary)
fabpedigree . com
66 Pope James (Saint)
(Half-brother of Jesus)
67 Jude (1st Apostle)
68 Elzasus
(Fredemundus 395-   )
69 Nascien I Desposyni
70 Celedoin   ca 440
71 Nascien II of Provinciae ca 465
72 Gallienus Quiriacus
73 Jonaans de Bretagne ca. 515

… to Matrilineal line (page 47)

Patrilinear:		Matrilinear:
104 Ere of Irish Dairiada		
105 Fergus Mor	c. 501	
106 Domangart	d. 506	
107 K. Gabran of Dairiada	d. 559	
108 Aedan Mac Gabran	d. 608	74 Ban (Bors) le Benoic
109 Eochaied Buide	d. 630	75 **Lancelot**, (Sir) le Benoic
110 Donald Brec	d. 642	76 Bors le Benoic
111 Domangart	d. 673	77 Lionel le Benoic
112 Eochaid "Crook Nose"	d. 696	78 Alain of Brittany
113 Findan		79 Froamidus of Brittany 8th C
114 Eochaid	d. 733	80 K. Frodaldus of Brittany
115 Aed the White	d. 778	81 Frotmund
116 Eochaid the Poisonous	d. 780	82 Flothair
117 Alpin of Kintyre	d. 834	83 Adelrad
118 K. Kenneth MacAlpin	810-858	84 Frotbald
119 King Aed	d. 878	85 Alirad
120 Doir	870-936	86 Frotmund
121 Murdoch	900-959	87 Fretaldus
122 Ferguard	929-980	88 Frotmaldus Vetules
123 Kenneth	960-1030	89 Fratmaldus Seneschal of Brittany
124 Banquo, Thane of Lochaber b. 990		90 Alan Seneschal of Dol 1020 -
125 Fleance, Thane of Lochaber b. 1020		91 Flaald Seneschal of Dol 1011-1076
126 Walter, Thane of Lochaber b. 1045		92 Alan FitzFlaald 1055-1121
127 Alan, Thane of Lochaber b. 1088 m.		93 Adelina of Oswestry

128 / 94 **Walter FitzAlan**	1106-1177 (1st High Steward)
129 / 95 **Alain FitzWalter**	1140-1204 (2nd High Steward)
130 / 96 **Walter Stewart**	1170-1246 (3rd High Steward)
131 / 97 **Alexander Stewart**	1214-1283 (4th High Steward)
132 / 98 **James Stewart**	1243*-1309 (5th High Steward)
133 / 99 **Walter Stewart**	1293-1327 (6th High Steward)

* Wikipedia dates are used as much as possible. James was possibly born as early as 1243, *before* the Seventh Crusade. See Stewart and Stewart, *The Stewarts of Appin,* page 38. See also www.geni.com/discussions/113421.

Don't you just love a mystery? Tracing the ancestry of our Stewart family presents us with several great mysteries. (Our lineage from Adam to Jonaans, through King David, can be seen above.) While the lines of the original High Stewards are clear, their offshoots have become muddied over time. Interestingly, however, we have some clues, and these lie with two of our Stewart ancestors, both of whom are named Alexander.

Our first Alexander (4th High Steward, 1214-1286) engendered separate lines of Stewarts. Alexander's first wife, Jean Macrory, gave birth to James of Dundonald (b. 1260, 5th High Steward), who married Gille de Burgh, giving rise to the line which I call the "High Road" (see the chart below). Their son Walter Stewart married Marjory Bruce, the only child of the famous Robert Bruce, and *their* (Walter and Marjory's) son became King Robert II of Scotland.

Another son of Alexander was Sir John Stewart (b. 1246), who married Margaret Bonkyl and became known as John of Bonkyl and Garlies. He became the progenitor of what I term the "Low Road." He was also the ancestor of King James VI (of Scotland) and I (of England).

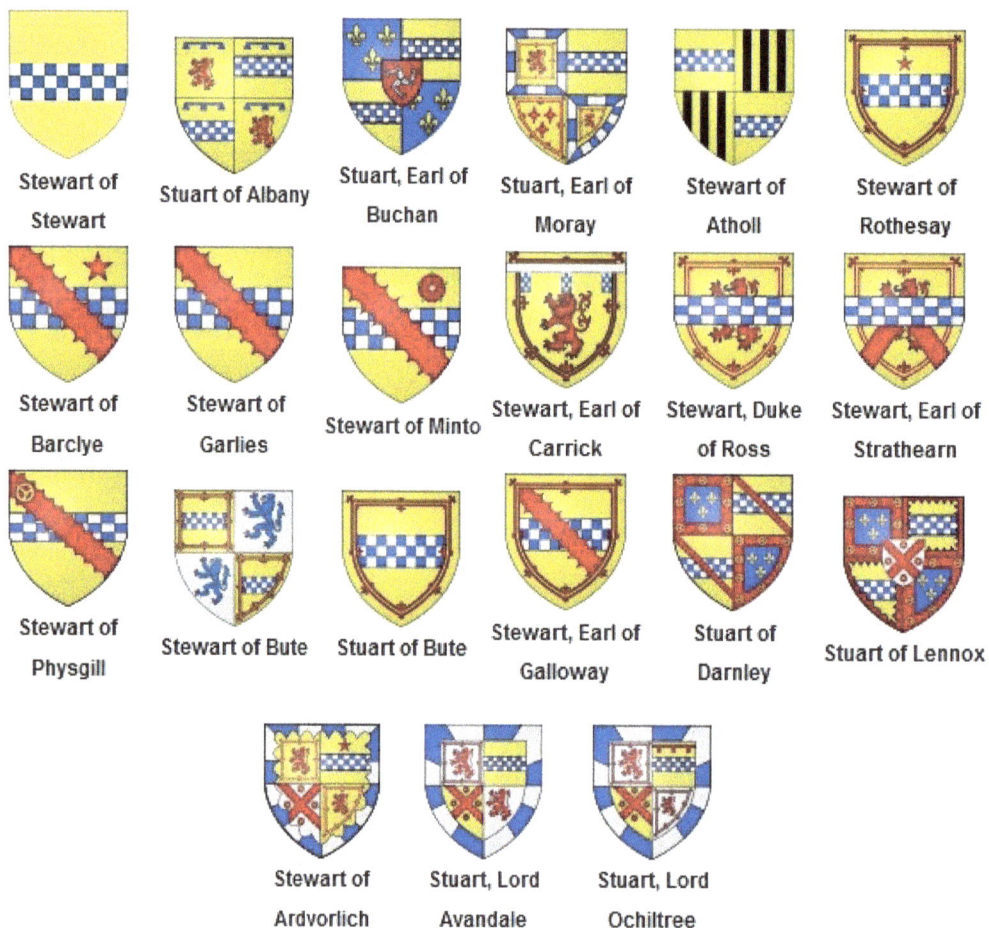

Stewart of Stewart

Stuart of Albany

Stuart, Earl of Buchan

Stuart, Earl of Moray

Stewart of Atholl

Stewart of Rothesay

Stewart of Barclye

Stewart of Garlies

Stewart of Minto

Stewart, Earl of Carrick

Stewart, Duke of Ross

Stewart, Earl of Strathearn

Stewart of Physgill

Stewart of Bute

Stuart of Bute

Stewart, Earl of Galloway

Stuart of Darnley

Stuart of Lennox

Stewart of Ardvorlich

Stuart, Lord Avandale

Stuart, Lord Ochiltree

	The "High Road"	The "Low Road
132	98 James of Dundonald 1260-1309 5th High Steward m. Gille de Burgh	98 Sir John Stewart of B & G 1246-1298 m. Margaret of Bonkyl & Garlies
133	99 Walter Stewart 6th H.S. 1293-1327 m. Princess Marjory Bruce	99 James Stewart of Pierston 1276-1333 m. Unknown
134	100 Robert II King of Scots 1316-90 m. Elizabeth Mure of Rowallan dtr – Margaret m. John of Islay	100 Robert Stewart, Shambothy & I-M 1310-1388 m. Catherine MacDougall
135	101 Robert Duke of Albany 1340-1420 m. Margaret Graham	101 John Stewart of Innermeath, Lorn 1348-1421 m. Isabel MacDougall
136	102 Murdoch, Duke Albany 1362-1425 m. Isabella Ctss. of Lennox	102 Alexander Stewart 2nd Grantully 1380-1449 m. Margaret Hay
137	103 Walter of Lennox 1394-1425 m. Janet Erskine	103 Thomas Steuart 3rd Grantully 1405-1462 m. Maud
138	104 James Mor 1400-1451 (Partner) Lady MacDonald	104 Alexander Stewart 4th Grantully 1430-1488 m. Matilda
139	105 Walter of Morphie 1425-1488 m. Elizabeth Arnot	105 John Steuart 5th Laird of Grantully 1432-1488 m.
140	106 Alexander L Avondale 1446-1489 m.	106 Alexander Steuart 7th Grantully 1470- m. Margaret Murray
141	107 Andrew 1st L Avondale 1470-1513 m. Margaret Kennedy	107 Thomas Steuart 8th Grantully 1495-1558 m. Mariota Murray
142	108 Sir James of Beith 1506 – 1544 m. Margaret Lindsay, L. Innermeath	108 William Steuart 9th Grantully 1516-1574 m. Margaret Abercrombie
143	109 James 1st Lord Donne 1529-90 m. Margaret Campbell	109 Thomas Steuart 10th Grantully 1543-1610 m. Grizel Mercer
144	110 James 2nd Earl Moray 1565-1592 "The Bonnie Earl O'Moray" m. Elizabeth Stewart Ctss. Moray	110 Donald Stewart 1570-1600 m. Catherine Mary Campbell
145	111 James 3rd Earl Moray 1581-1638 m. Anne Gordon	111 Duncan Stewart 1595-1655 m. Helen Margaret Campbell
146	112 James 4th Earl Moray 1608-1653 m. Margaret Home	112 **Alexander Stewart** 1634-1731 m. **Hannah Templar**
147	113 Alexander 5 Earl Moray 1634-1701 m. Emilia Balfour	

Far left column continued from page 47 (Patrilineal, High Stewards) above.

Our latest Alexander (1634-1731, #114 [not listed] or #112) also created confusion. Who was he? Was he a son of Alexander, the 5th Earl of Moray, who came to America with his brother Duncan? Or was he a son of Duncan and Helen, a PoW of the English Civil War?

Then there is the problem of Alexander's wife Hannah. Was her father's name Temple, or Templar, or both?

Finally, their son Dr. John Stewart. Why do most ancestry sites say that he was born in New York, while they all insist that Hannah, who was born and died in modern-day Massachusetts, was his mother? Were Alexander and Hannah both living in New York at one point?

These are some of the mysteries of the Stewart Clan.

148	113 Dr. John Stewart	m. Isabel Alberti
149	114 Samuel Stewart	m. Lydia Harrison
150	115 Joseph Stewart	m. Sarah Gilbert
151	116 Samuel P. Stewart	m. Polly Kitchner
152	117 David Kimbrough Stewart	m. Margaret Robertson
153	118 John Thomas Stewart	m. Louisa Ophelia McMillan
154	119 Alva Clinton Stewart	m. Minnie Evelyn Passmore
155	120 Leonard Jackson Stewart	m. Faye Marilyn Milor
156	121 Jan Eylander Jackson Stewart	m. Misa Abe

(The generation numbers at far left have been continued from the patrilineal chart on page 49, above. The numbers next to the names (#113, etc.) have been continued from the "Low Road."

11

*Lancelot**

ca. 520 ~

Birth and Childhood

Somewhere between Gaul and Brittany, in the Wood of Broceliande, I Galhadriel, son of King Ban of Benoic was born. In those days were petty wars fought between petty kings. My father was killed by a Frankish one as my mother Elaine looked on. While she tended her dying husband, I was carried off a-swaddling by Nimuec, who appeared to be a faerie.

Nimuec spirited me to her home by a lake in a faraway land. There she raised me to be her servant, and so she called me "l'Ancelot," which means "servant" in my native tongue.

Nimue la Fée

She was old as the heavy water
 That circles the earth,
Unswum by even the deepest fish,
 Yet comely as grain
 in the morning sun.

Her children *Merlin* and *Brisen* roamed
 The land in search of
 Lost children to save;
Taking them to the White Flower Close,
There to learn the ways of the Faerie.

'Twas providence, or "la voluptée" –
 She altered the shape
 Of the Pendragon,
To cloud the eyes of the forlorn queen,
 Then Arthur was born.

---

* Author's Note: Not much is known about the historical Lancelot, so I give you this piece about his great-grandson, the literary Lancelot.

He carried the child
>   To the Abbess of the White Flower,
>   There to await that fateful moment
> When sword from the stone
> He would forthwith draw.

Childhood Lessons

The ways of the Faerie were little known to me, but as I knew little else in the months leading up to my father's death, I could easily adapt. Once, when I was eight years old, my stepbrother instructed me to wrestle with seven lions. If I won the bout, he said, I would marry a princess when I grew up.

The lions released he, enclosed in a pen, and I the bold or foolish child did wrestle them one by one. Four by four I bound their paws with sheep shank knots, until all seven were defeated. It was only then that my sergeant-at-arms revealed his ruse – his "lions" were lambs, each wearing a skin that he had fashioned out of cord-du-roi.

Little did I know that his promise of marrying a princess would come true, but only inasmuch as his trick of the lion skins would allow.

Excalibur is Broken

As I grew strong and became a man, my Lady of the Lake fashioned for me a shirt of mail, seamless and fine as cloth, yet indestructible. A suit of armor worn over it was naught but ornament. One day as I lay sunning myself in a meadow beside a stream, there came a company of riders, one of whom appeared to be their king. Their banners and coronets proved it.

"Stand aside and let us pass," said their king, confident in his own righteousness. "We are surveying this land, for all that I see is mine."

"Nay, I will not," said I, for beyond was my Lady's lake, which she commanded me to guard. "O'er my mother's realm no king reigns. You may take the long way around if you wish to pass."

"Yield, or you shall taste my sword, Excalibur," said he, weary of his travels, "against which the gates of Hell shall not prevail."

"Nay, I shall not," I rejoined, for I feared my Mistress more than I feared his charming Sword. "But first let us joust. Yonder stand my lances; make good use of one, Sir."

So we jousted, until one unseated the other, at which time we met on edges. We parried and feinted, then we struck each other blows, until at last he got lucky and landed his blade on my own shoulder. It did not hurt…it did not bleed… but his precious Excalibur broke in two.

He tore off his face guard, and with tears in his eyes exclaimed, "How can this be so? My sword was invincible! What manner of knight or fiend are you?"

I explained that I was neither knight nor fiend, that I was only a boy set to guard my mother's lands, and that I regretted breaking so splendid a sword, and I offered to pay for it seven crowns.

"Never mind," said the King. "My own pride hath defeated me. We shall not intrude on thy mother's abode, but rather, though weary, take the long way around."

And with that he and his company turned and essayed not to cross the bridge over my mother's stream, though he threw the pieces of his broken sword therein. I watched in wonder as the riders receded into the distance, banners and coronets waving in the breeze.

The Ring of Choirs

When my face grew fur my stepmother took me to Logres, the realm of the king, seeking to procure my knighthood. As we came into that fabled land, we passed by the close at Uttoxeter. There, as in numerous other cloisters, one hundred voices sang, with each hour a changing came, so in one day 2,400 voices were heard. With each season, their songs echoed the changing of the stars. Together the numerous cloisters formed a protective circle around their lustrous city, Camelot. Such was the Kingdom of Logres.

Guinevere

We came at last to their city, the most splendid sight that eyes could see, arrayed in silver and stone, but I was unlucky on that day, for I chanced to see a frog in a ditch beside the road. (People who dwell in lakes are unlucky to look on a frog.) It was not your everyday run-of-the mill frog, for it had the face of a woman – the king's sister Morgan.

Nimuec had healed the king's sword which he threw in her stream. Now she brought it as ransom to persuade the king to grant me knighthood. That he did, on the provision that I take part in his tournament, to be held three days thence.

We entered the hall on white horseback, not to be swayed by its guards. The squires took our steeds, and my mother took me to the court. A ring she gave me to ward off enchantments, but it was too late; the roadside frog had already done its harm.

As I sat at the Round Table, knights greeted knights, and I the initiate, wondered at this blessing. Yet sometimes a blessing turns to a curse: the queen then dared to enter the court. Her eyes met mine in the instant she spoke. I was lost to a love that I could not define, nor requite.

The tournament came and went, but I could think of nothing besides fair Guinevere, who watched from her gallery. The first day I was the Black Knight; the second day, Red; the third, White. Gawain, the king's nephew, could not best me in jousting, nor mace, nor swordplay. Yet he was the better knight than I: he wore the garter to prove it.

The Land of Moribund

One dark night a courtier appeared in our midst, telling us that the queen had been taken to the Land of Moribund. "Who will champion Guinevere?" the king asked. Of course, it was I who would go to her aid, though Gawain had such hopes, as well.

Halfway there, I stopped at a chapel to pray. When my prayers were finished, I looked up to see a young girl, all dressed in white. "Sir, your horse has expired," she said. It was true: outside I found my mount lying sideways on the street.

Perchance a dwarf approached driving a *corbillard*.* He offered to give me a ride to the Land of Moribund, but I hesitated. He offered a second time; again, I hesitated. At last I accepted and climbed aboard his cart.

The Land of Moribund was ghastly as winter, where no leaves grew on the trees. Corbies rested on withered branches. Mud and slime covered our tracks. When at last the dwarf let me off, I found myself in the Castle of Doom. Its keeper required me to unburden myself of all appurtenances.

Inside, fair Guinevere wore a garment of black. She embroidered a cloak with a message of foreboding. "What took you so long?" she demanded.

"M'lady, I came as quickly…" came my reply.

"Nay, twice you hesitated to mount the dwarf's wagon," she said, correctly accusing me.

"I am sorry. Please forgive me."

She slapped me lightly on the cheek, then she forgave me.

Betrayal

We emerged from that Dismal Dungeon, the one where my fair queen had been held, though not entirely against her will. On the way back to Logres we stopped for a rest at the castle of King Pelles in Corbenic.

There the evil Morgan le Fay did attempt to persuade me, but I from my vows of knighthood did not swerve. In the Land of Moribund I had relinquished my mother's ring; now I lay exposed to the guile of the enchantress. At night she veiled my eyes: I believed this other was Guinevere, and softly I kissed her.

* A hearse.

'Twas not. To my horror I awoke and found by my side fair Helayne, daughter of our host King Pelles. I had betrayed my King. I had betrayed my Queen. I had betrayed my knightly Brothers. I had betrayed myself. I had betrayed our host, and I had defiled his daughter.

Driven mad by my own wickedness, I roamed the forest in the form of a wolf for the duration of her fullness. In the dead of my winter, by fortune Nimuec found me, and by her touch healed me. Then at King Pelles' castle I saw the child Galahad once, but Brisen spirited the child away to be raised in the Abbey of the White Flower.

Now I am old and retired to my priory, as Guinevere has to her abbey. My knightly companions instructed have I, to liquidate all my inheritance. If all is done that I asked, should they find in their bodies strength, to go to the Holy Land, there to drive from the Temple Mount the Saracens, restoring the Land to the Faith.

12

Walter FitzAlan

First High Steward

ca. 1106-1177

When I was a wee lad of eight, my father sent me to live with the hounds. "There is no better way to become a man," he said, "than to live a dog's life." I protested, but he told me a boy had no place in the kitchen. From that day forward, I thought as a hound, I spake as a hound, I ate as a hound. My mother, sweet Adelina, sent cakes to tide me over.

The next year, he sent me to live in the stable. "There is no better way to become a sire, than to know the life of the mare." *Equus. Cheval. Steed. Horse.* I learned how to whisper with the tongues of men and of angels. Sweet Adelina sent me berries and honey.

On my first hunt, at fifteen years of age, I went with the king's *Luparii*, the wolf patrol. Most of my companions were servants, all dressed in green. That same winter I hunted the boar, all dressed in gray. By then I had mastered the horseback, so my noble companions allowed me the privilege of lancing the beast when it was cornered.

The Stag is Dead; Long Live the Stag!

I finally turned sixteen, the legal age of the stag-hunting master. We had a saying: "If you want to live to ninety-nine, wake up at five, break fast at nine; have supper at five, go to bed at nine!" I always thought that with so many fives and nines, living like that would only get you to fifty-nine! Anyway, hunting was risky business. You could get killed by a stag, or a wolf, or a boar, though probably not by a hare. I still had to wake up at five to go to the hunt.

The Quest. Our "Questing Beast" had already gone out and come back. He was a man, but I called him a beast because he was not of Breton stock; he was one of the Celtic tribes who stayed on after we arrived in England. Perhaps his people were once Druids, so he had a knack for seeking out the quarry. He talked to the foresters and woodsmen. He found tracks, broken branches with patches of fur, and droppings. He worked his magic. He found the overnight lay of the stag and marked the trails in and out.

Preparations. I put on my red tunic and high boots to protect my legs from burrs and twigs while chasing through the woods. My "unicorn" (one-pointed) cap fit me like a glove. I carried my saber and dagger in my belt, my hunting horn slung over my shoulder. On my left hand, a glove; in my bare right hand a leather thong to strike against my boot, to call the hounds.

The Gathering. The table with cloth was set in the park. Breakfast was served: we broke bread together and ate it with cheese made from deer's milk. We examined the droppings and planned our approach. The Questing Beast had cut a small stick to the size of the hoofprints. We chose to pursue a five-year-old stag and swore not to be distracted by other animals that we should encounter.

Along the paths to the stag's lay, the hounds waited in groups of three, for to run in **relays**. The greyhounds, you see, were good at the sprint, but they needed to rest; the Stag had more stamina.

The Fynding. Our lymer* set out to track down the stag. It sniffed along the trail, turning hither and thither, until there, in a clearing, stood the Stag, snorting from its nostrils into a hole in the ground. Out came a serpent, gasping for air, at which sight the Stag with its hooves trampled the viper to death.

The Chase. *Tu-whoo!* The chase was on. Each blast of the horn was met with resound, significance, meaning, known to all as we rode. The hounds bore down on the scent of the Stag. Over hill and under branch they chased him, but they could not keep up with the lusty Stag.

Then at once the Stag himself seemed to tire. He could not sweat, so he stopped to rest in a pool beneath a waterfall. Not one to be taken by hounds, he got up and resumed the chase.

The Baying. They had cornered the beast near a thicket. Then the Stag turned to defend itself, but the hounds kept him at bay. Nothing he could do to escape them, though he gored one or two and they were lost. *Tu-whoo!* Call off your hounds! It is time for the sword or the spear.

At length I caught up with the pack. One of the hunters played a tone on his reed pipe to transfix the Stag.

The Kill. I dismounted and drew my saber. This was the moment of truth. Kill or be killed. I looked the Stag in the eye. He charged, antlers down, ready to disembowel me, to draw me and quarter me there for all my underlings to see.

* A special tracking dog, a bloodhound, always kept on a "lyme," or line. (Fleance, Walter's grandfather, had the nickname *Flann* – "bloodhound.")

No! Just as he made his final lunge, I reached over his antlers and drove my saber down between his shoulder blades! He stopped in his tracks. I stood at attention and doffed my cap to him, first directly in front, then to my left, then extending it to my right as far as my arm could reach. As he turned his head from right to left to follow the movement of my cap, he severed his own spinal cord with the blade of my saber. He dropped to his knees helpless.

I put my left hand on his face and walked around to his left side, all the time looking him straight in the eye. They say that on your first hunt you can see the sign of the Cross between a stag's antlers as you kill it. I saw much more than that. With my right hand, I drew my dagger and thrust it up under the Stag's rib cage into his heart. At the moment I felt its tip scrape against his heart bone, all time was suspended. During that moment the very light of God Eternal shone down on me through his eye. I will never forget what I saw that day, it had such a great impact on my life.

I fell to my knees. The death of the Stag had transformed me. All who were present, whether man or horse or hound, also fell to their knees. We men blew our horns, and the hounds howled. *Tu-WHOOOOo. Tu-WHOOOOo. Tu-WHOOOOo. The Stag is dead! Long live the Stag!*

Then from behind, my attendants came and placed a white cloak on my shoulders, a white cap on my head, the same as they wore. With much ceremony, one drew the dagger from out of the Stag's breast. According to the creed of Saint Hubert, he made the sign of the Cross on my forehead with the blood of the Stag's heart. Then he did the same on my right cheek and on my left cheek. I was washed in the Blood of the Stag.

We played a fanfare on our horns. *Tu-Whoo!* Then began **the Unmaking.** "I will now unmake you," I said solemnly, but in fact it was my companions who performed this task.

First came the undoing. They split the deer apart, slit its midsection, and removed its entrails. Then came the fleaning. They flayed the animal and skinned it. Then came the brittling. They cut it into pieces.

Finally, we performed **the Curée.** In this ceremony we gave the hounds their reward, making sure to associate it with the hunt. The servants stretched out the hide of what once was the Stag on the ground. Then they placed the kidneys, lungs, paunch, and windpipe upon it, and mixed the pieces with blood.

On that day the Stag, conceived at the rising of Arcturus, the master of the forest, became venison. I, conceived of the flesh and master of the kitchen, became a man of God. One day I would hunt the Unicorn.

Birth and Good Fortune

I was born in Oswestry, England, a suburb of Shropshire. My grandfather was Alan FitzFlaald (funny name, isn't it?), and my mother was Adelina de Hesdin. Before he came to England, my grandfather had been a steward to the bishops of Dol in Brittany. When Henry, son of William the Conqueror, was besieged by his brothers at Mont-Saint-Michel (1091), my grandfather helped him. We Seneschals of Dol knew every nook and cranny of Mont-Saint-Michel (there was a secret door that could only be accessed at low tide). Gramdfather smuggled in supplies and water when Henry's brothers weren't looking. When Henry became king of England in 1100 (his older brother was killed in a hunting accident), he granted my grandfather lands in Shropshire.

Our "good fortune" began when King Henry's son drowned in the White Ship accident. This threw confusion on the kingdom, for he was the only male heir to the throne. In desperation, Henry appointed his daughter Matilda to succeed him, but he knew this wouldn't go over well.

In 1135, Henry ate too many lampreys and died. By this time Matilda and her new husband Geoffrey of Anjou were rebelling against him, and she tried to seize the throne. Stephen of Blois (who had conveniently disembarked the fated White Ship before it sailed) seized the throne in England. We sided with David (brother of Henry' widow Matilda), who became King of Scotland.

A year later, King David I offered me a substantial grant of lands, in exchange for the service of several knights for each property. I had two capitals: one at Dundonald and the other at Renfrew. I also had to command my knights in battle.

SIGILLUM WALTERI FILII
ALANI DAPIFERI REG
Seal of Walter son of Alan,
Steward of the King

When it came to combat, I was good with a lance (after all, I had once killed a wild boar, hadn't I?). Our cousins the Normans had started using the stirrup, so we could ride our horses straight into battle, instead of jumping off as the Norsemen did. I was also getting pretty good at using the arming sword. In 1147 I took part in the Siege of Lisbon, in which we expelled the Moors. Then in 1160 I helped King Malcom IV invade Galloway. I also led the defense against Somerled, the King of the Isles. He came at us (actually, his target was me) with forces drawn from Argyll, Dublin, and the Isles, and landed at Renfrew. We pushed him back (which is a nice way of saying, we killed him).

As a reward for my services, I became the king's *dapifer* (steward) and held that office even when King Malcom died, and William became king. As steward, I was responsible for the day-to-day running of the king's household (his hall – the chamberlain took care of his sleeping quarters). The butler took care of his wine; the constable commanded the king's knights.

When I was still a young man (1131), I married Eschina (de Molle) of London. We had two daughters named Margaret and Christina ('44), and three sons named **Alan** ('40), Walter (d. 1167), and Simon.

FitzAlan

Londres

In 1163 I founded Paisley Priory in the barony of Renfrew. Later it was moved to Paisley proper, and it became an abbey. The abbey still stands as you, gentle reader, read my story.

The Butcher of Rouen

'Twas in one dark November,
That fated ship set sail;
The one they called the White Ship,
Had weathered wind and gale;
Whose captain never faltered,
Except this one last time;
When wood and canvas slipped beneath
The Channel's foaming brine.

The night before we sailed with
The Bonny Prince aboard,
I went to the Cathedral and
Beseeched our Saving Lord:
Oh, Christ, Oh Saints, protect us,
On bended knees, *toujours*,
Tomorrow as we venture from
The docks of Port Barfleur.

Our king had left before us,
On his much slower *barque*,
Our crew first quaffed a wine-fest,
Then strove to overtake his ark.
'Twas then we struck the *Quilleboeuf*,
That rock its target found;
The Bonny Prince turned back to save
His sister; both were drowned.

And now, three hundred souls are gone,
Save I, the Butcher of Rouen.

13

Alain FitzWalter

Second High Steward

1140-1204

It was Saladin who caused this third Crusade. He made himself Sultan of Egypt, then he united the Moslems in Syria and marched against the Kingdom of Jerusalem. Even the Holy Cross was lost in the Battle of Galilee.

In every corner of Christendom, men began sewing the cross on their garments – in gold if they could afford it, in silk if they were of the merchant class, or in plain cloth if they were peasants. Most famous and fearsome were the red crosses of the Knights Templar.

So it was that vows of chastity, poverty, and obedience gained a newborn friend: the Templars vowed to protect pilgrims and fight the infidels. The Templars not only protected pilgrims, but also acted as bankers, and soon became very wealthy as a result. The Knights Hospitaller vowed to care for sick pilgrims in Jerusalem. The Teutonic Knights split from this movement to begin their own order of Germans. You could easily recognize them by their white cloak with a black cross on the left shoulder.

Now the German Emperor Frederick, though nearly seventy years old, set out to fight the Turks. Some say he was drowned while crossing a swollen stream; he had to abandon his crusader spirit.

The English and French kings had better luck. Sending more than half a million men, they finally took the city of Acre after a long siege. But both kings quarreled, and Philip finally went home to France.

For two years King Richard the Lion-Hearted fought with his gracious host Saladin for control of Jerusalem. I joined him in 1191. Unfortunately, neither side won the war. We let Saladin keep control Jerusalem, provided he would let Christian pilgrims visit without paying tribute.

On his way home, poor Richard was shipwrecked and captured by the Duke of Austria. His ransom was more than twice the GNP of England. When I got back, I vowed to help the Knights Templar in Scotland. With my help they acquired land in Roslin, in hopes of building their own church there one day.

Marriage(s) and Family

I had three wives (not at the same time, of course). Alesta was the daughter of Morggan of Mar. Eva Crawford was a different story: she was a granddaughter of Thor. Finally, Margaret Galloway, a daughter of Fergus Molle and Elizabeth FitzHenry of Normandy.

I didn't want to cause any internecine squabbles, so I treated all my children as equal offspring of all my wives. Their names were **Walter** ('70) of Dundonald, William, David ('83), Leonard ('85), Simon ('75), and Avelina ('79). The only thing I will tell you about them is that Avelina married Alesta's brother Donnchad, so you can guess that Alesta was not her mother.

I was twenty-seven when my father died. Then I inherited his title, High Steward of Scotland. When I came back from the Crusade in 1191, I became a patron of the Knights Templar and helped expand their influence in Scotland. They had lands in Roslin, south of Edinburgh, where they planned one day to build a church.

SIGILL ALANI FILII WALTERI
Seal of Alan son of Walter

In 1192, Angus mac Somerled defeated his brother Ragnall (Reginald, "rex insularim"), who made an offering to Paisley Abbey (founded by my father) to try to gain my support. He offered to pay an annual sum of one penny for every house in his lands with a hearth. I took him up on his offer, and eventually I became Lord of the Isle of Bute. There I built a Norman-style church. This made King William (of Scotland) nervous, so he built a castle at Ayr to prevent me from increasing control of lands to the south of Renfrew. While William was away in England, I arranged for my daughter Avelina to marry Donnchad, Earl of Carrick.

14

Walter Stewart

Third High Steward

ca. 1170-1246

You may wonder why I took the name *Stewart*. Before my grandfather came over here, we were *dapifers* – *seneschals*. Well, I was born here in Scotland, a third-generation immigrant. It was time to assimilate, so I took on a Scottish surname.*

It was all about *bon gout* ("good taste"), you see. King David (not the one who slew Goliath) invited my grandfather to come over from France, and with good reason. He wanted to replace the "food-divider" (Gaelic *rannaire*) with a full-fledged *steward* who would take care of the king's hall. We were the royal caterers, running the king's day-to-day business of eating.

Three kings later (Alexander II, r. 1214-1249), crusaders like my father brought back pepper and spices from the Near East. Salt was expensive, but necessary to preserve meat to eat in winter. We used honey as a sweetener.

The original inhabitants of Britain were not good cooks at all. They didn't use oil, and they didn't use butter. They couldn't eat sheep or rabbits, hens or geese, or even fish, because of their superstitions.

The Norsemen, who came later, loved their great-hall feasts but there was no elegance in their manner of eating, nor of their cooking. (They did bring Angus beef with them, so maybe we can overlook some of their improprieties.) What we found here after the Conquest was a nation prone to drunkenness and gluttony.

The Scottish kings have always liked to hunt – not only boar and deer, but also rabbit, grouse, peacocks and swans. Meals were topped off with cabbage, beans, turnips, carrots, and maybe a bit of wild garlic. The Church wouldn't let anyone eat meat on Wednesdays, Fridays and Saturdays, so they had to eat fish.

We of the Continent brought with us a more delicate eating style (*delicat-essen*, as our Frankish neighbors would say). This good taste was a long time in the making.

We Dapifers held a high office in Brittany. In the monasteries, the Cellarer supervised the cooks, though the Lardyrer was the chief cook. All were under our supervision.

* From Old English "stig-weard" = household + guardian.

Let's take a look at some of the duties of the Lord High Steward of Scotland. Down in the castle kitchens a small army prepared the food. The *Magister Coquina*, an esquire by rank, was in charge of all of them. Larderers made sure the kitchens were well-stocked. Fruit and vegetables were gathered from the castle orchards and gardens. Poulters prepared the birds. The cook led the undercooks and bakers, who made fresh bread in huge ovens.

We had knives and spoons, but no forks (those were invented later by Italians, who ate noodles). Norman plates were made of wood. We sometimes used large slices of day-old bread for the meat; sometimes we ate out of bowls.

The Walter Stewart Cookbook

Now, let us take a look at our innovative style. After all, the reason King Henry brought my grandfather here in the first place was to improve the quality of dining.

The Scots liked to eat all kinds of disgusting things (I almost have to hold my nose while I tell you about them):

- Turtle Soup. A dish to enjoy on special occasions. Made from real turtles.
- Brain Cakes. Leftovers from sheep brain broth, made into cakes.
- Puffins. Eaten as a snack (I hear the MacLeods accepted puffin feathers as partial payment of rent).
- Caudell. Wine thickened with egg yolks; sugar added.
- Cockatrice. Half serpent, half rooster. The recipe called for half a chicken to be sewn onto half a roast suckling pig.

Our Norman meals are chiefly soups, potages, *ragouts*, hashes, and hodge-podges. Entire joints of meat are never served, and animals or fowl are seldom brought to the table whole, but hacked, hewed, or cut in pieces. They are eaten with a spoon or the fingers. We use a finger bowl before eating; we dip our hands in perfumed Damask water after dinner.

We have a great regard for the eye, as well as the palate. We even use gilded or silvered leaves of trees to ornament our plates. Here are some examples of our menu. I put them in alphabetical order, for your convenience.

Almond Milk Rice.   Rice comes from far away, so only the King can afford it. This dish is basically a rice pudding. Cook the rice, drain it, and leave it in a saucepan. Cover with almond milk, then simmer. Add honey, sugar, and cook the whole mixture until thick.

Apple Muse. Take apples and boyle them, strain them into a pot. Then take almond milk and honey, add grated bread, saffron, sandalwood and a little salt. Put into a pot and let it boil. Add honey. Stir well.

Compost. This is the closest thing the King gets to peasant food, but with a much richer sauce. Basically, you throw all your leftover vegetables in a crock-pot and leave them to simmer. Put in parsley roots, carrots, parsnips, turnips, radishes, cabbage, and pears; dice and boil them until soft. Sprinkle with salt and allow to cool. Serve with pepper, saffron, and vinegar.

Cormarye. This is a big hunk of pork in rich sauce. Make a sauce from red wine, ground pepper, garlic, coriander, caraway seeds and salt. Roast a pork joint in it. Add sauce and drippings to a broth and serve them together.

Cryspes (Crepes). Moisten flour with egg yolks and whites. Beat together for a long time. Put lard on the fire in a little iron pan, let it bubble, then take a bowl pierced with a hole as wide as your finger, put the batter in the dish. Let it flow all over the pan. Then put a plate with powdered sugar on top.

Funges. Cut mushrooms and leeks into small pieces and add to a broth, with saffron for coloring. "Powder fort" is a spice mixture made from pepper and ginger or cinnamon. Add cloves.

Payn Ragoun.   This is a fudge-like candy, served alongside meat or fish rather than as dessert. Flavors include rose and citrus. Use muffin tins. Take honey and sugar and clarify it, stirring frequently over low heat. Brush down sugar granules with a pastry brush. Heat it, cool a little in a pot, under cold water. Add ground ginger then beat it. Stir in pine nuts. Let it cool.

Payn Fondew. This is a type of bread pudding. Fry bread in grease. Mix egg whites in red wine. Add raisins, honey, sugar, cinnamon, ginger, cloves, and simmer until thick. Break up the bread, add it to the syrup, and let it soak. Sprinkle with coriander and sugar.

Toastie. This is more like jam on toast. Mix red wine and honey in a saucepan. Add ground ginger, salt, and pepper. Cook until thick. Spoon over toasted bread. Chop up some fresh ginger and sprinkle on top.

Venison Y-bake. Take hocks of venison, boil in salted water. When done, make pastry dough and put the venison on it. Cover above and beneath with pepper, ginger, and salt, then set in the oven, bake with honey and serve.

Verde Sawse. This is like green salsa. Mix parsley, mint, garlic, thyme, sage, cinnamon, ginger, and pepper with wine. Add to breadcrumbs, vinegar, and salt mixed together. Serve as is.

At the turn of the century I married Bethoc (Beatrix) nic Gille Crist, Countess of Angus.

Stewart

Angus

Our children were Euphemia ('01), Sybella ('05), Margaret ('06), Beatrix ('10), **Alexander** ('14, 4th High Steward), John ('16, killed in Damietta, Egypt), Walter Bailloch "The Freckled" ('18), and Robert ('23) of Tarbolten and Crookston.

15

Alexander Stewart

Fourth High Steward

1214-1283

In my thirty-fourth year I went on a crusade. Jerusalem had once more returned to Musselman control in 1244. The Pope called for another crusade, but no one responded. The only king interested in a crusade was Louis IX of France.

We sailed 15,000 strong in thirty-six ships, specially built. After wintering in Cyprus, we promised to help recover Byzantium, Nicaea, Antioch, and Sidon. To this end Louis landed at Damietta on the Nile. He thought Egypt would provide a solid base from which to attack Jerusalem.

The Seventh Crusade

We took Damietta with little resistance. Soon the Nile flooded, so we were grounded for six months. In November we marched towards Cairo, only to be defeated by the Mamaluks, but then we laid siege to a town called Mansourah. It was a disaster. One of my Templar friends wrote home to his brothers:

"It seems that God wishes to support the Turks rather than the Christians. I am afraid the East will never rise again; they will turn Holy Mary's convent into a mosque. God, who was once awake, must be sleeping now, for Mohammed waxes powerful."

We finally headed back to Damietta, but our army was annihilated. My brother John was killed in the fight by a Saracen named Massour. Louis came down with dysentery and had to be treated by an Arab physician. Then he was taken captive. His ransom: 800,000 *bezants* *, plus the surrender of Damietta.

Though our Crusade ended in failure, Louis received a hero's welcome when he returned to France. A noble effort. Troubadours sang his praises, and many considered him a saint.

Shortly before I went on this crusade (1240), I had married Jean Macrory, heiress of the Isles of Bute and Arran. We had six children – Alianor ('39), **James** ('43), to whom I later passed the Stewardship of Scotland, John ('46), Mary ('47), Hawise ('49) and Elisabeth ('50). Beatrix ('68) and Andrew ('78) were born after I came back from the Crusade.

Stewart

Macrory

* Author's Note: A *bezant* (from "Byzantium," ancient name for Constantinople, now called Istanbul) was a gold *dinar* coin minted by Islamic governments. It weighed one *mithqal* (4.25 grams = 0.13664 Troy ounce). Louis' ransom was 109,312 ounces.

16

James Stewart

Fifth High Steward

1243-1309

My father had planned a pilgrimage to the shrine of Saint James of Compostela* in 1252. That is probably why he named me James, instead of Walter or Alan, as was common in our family.

In 1286 I became one of the six Regents of Scotland. As such, I had to submit to King Edward I of England, but why not? When my father died five years earlier, I had become the High Steward of Scotland. (Later I changed my mind and supported Robert the Bruce, of Scotland.)

In 1302 I was sent to solicit the aid of the French king against Edward. This was a bit tricky because Edward's son was betrothed to Princess Isabella of France. (But Edward Junior was madly in love with a man named Piers Gaveston… perhaps we could make use of that?)

As for me, I married three times: first to Cecilia of Dunbar; next to Muriel of Strathearn; lastly to Gille de Burgh of Ulster. Gille and I had five children: **Walter** ('93, 6th High Steward), Sir John ('94), Sir Andrew ('95), Gilles "Egidia" ('96), and Sir James of Durisdeer ('98).

* Author's Note: In 813, a hermit heard music in a forest and saw a shining light (*stella* in Spanish) above and somehow connected this to Saint James the Apostle. News of this revelation reached Bishop Teodomiro, who ordered an investigation that led to the discovery of the Apostle's relics. King Alfonso II then declared Saint James to be the patron saint of Spain and had a chapel built at the site (*Campus Stellae* --> *Compostela*). Pilgrims coming from Portugal after the Moors were driven out in the 12th century followed the *Camino de Santiago* ("Road of Saint James").

17

Walter Stewart

Sixth High Steward

ca. 1293-1327

At the crossroads of Renfrew Road and Dundonald Street stands a cairn marking the place where I, while great with child, fell off my horse and died. Of all things. Couldn't they have chosen something a bit more cheerful to remember me by? Well, I guess our son Robert survived the crash, and indeed he went on to become King of Scotland... if that is any consolation to me.

My name is Marjory Stewart. I was born in 1296, daughter of Robert the Bruce, Lord of Annandale and Earl of Carrick. My mother, Isabella de Mar, died when I was born (I think it was some sort of witchcraft: a midwife, who belongs to the cult of Diana and thinks she can fly, placed a curse on our family for as long as she lives... I hope she doesn't live too long).

When I was six, my father married Elizabeth de Burgh, whose father was Earl of Ulster. Two years later my father's rival was murdered (they made it look like my father did it), so he had himself crowned King of Scotland. This made King Edward of England furious.

In 1306 the English army came to punish my father, so we had to run away. I was sent north, along with my stepmother and my aunts, hoping to take refuge in the Orkneys, or further away in Norway, but we were captured while waiting for a boat.

Aunt Mary was locked in a cage and hung from the walls of Roxburgh castle. Is that any way to treat a lady? My stepmother Elizabeth was confined to various manors and treated more kindly, because the King didn't want to ruffle her father's feathers too much. As for me, they constructed a cage at the Tower of London, but the King decided not to abuse a child in such a way, so he sent

73

me to Watton Abbey in Yorkshire, where I was imprisoned for eight years.

Finally, in 1314, Edward sent his son (also named Edward) to fight with my father at Bannockburn. My father won and took a lot of English noblemen hostage. We were set free in a prisoner exchange. I was by that time seventeen years old.

My father sent Walter Stewart, a distinguished "commander" at the battle of Bannockburn, to escort me and the others home from English captivity. What a charming man! He later asked my father for my hand in marriage! Granted! We were married the following year. (Part of my dowry was the castle and Barony of Bathgate in Midlothian.)

Walter didn't really need another castle, nor a barony. He was already High Steward of Scotland, with castles at Renfrew and Dundonald. Three years after I died, King Edward II laid siege to Berwick while my father was away in Ireland, but my husband destroyed some of their siege engines. A few years after that, my father and his comrades pursued King Edward the younger towards York with 500 horsemen. He got away, but what a chase!

Speaking of horses… mine was named Knocker. What a fine steed! One day in early spring I decided to go out for a ride near Paisley Abbey, but something darted across the trail in front of us. Knocker bolted and threw me to the ground. The monks cut the child from my womb… I watched the whole thing. It didn't hurt a bit, surprisingly, but it seemed like I was watching them from above. I was lying on the ground, motionless. "I ken it is a laddie," I said (famous last words).

I hear that my granddaughter Margaret married a man named MacDonald, King of the Isles.

74

Part 2
The Distaff Side

Up to this point I have concentrated on the Stewarts, starting with those who first came to the New World, then briefly looking into the lives of those first caretakers of Scotland, the ones who first began to use the surname *Stewart*.

Along the way, I began to notice the stories of some of the women whom these early Stewarts married. While it is not practical, space-wise, to investigate every single branch of every family tree (see Section 3 below – How Many Ancestors?), several of them are very interesting, so let's digress for a while!

I will begin with Hannah Templar, who married our first American progenitor, Alexander Stewart. Following her family "tree" will lead us deep into the roots of Saxon England and beyond. A step in the opposite direction leads us to one of Hannah's daughters-in-law, a descendant of the first Italian immigrant to the New World.

After that I will spend some time with the maternal ancestors of my paternal grandmother (the Bantas), one of them another early inhabitant of New Amsterdam; then of *her* paternal line (the Passmores), which will lead us back to Jamestown.

Lastly, I will delve into the lives of my own mother's family. Although this branch of the family tree cannot be traced very far, it is indeed one of the most interesting.

Happy reading!

The Temples

Temple

This Anglo-Saxon name comes from the family that resided close to the temple, which originally belonged to the Knights Templar. The Templars had several houses, one at Temple Church, London; another in the parish of Temple in Edinburgh; the most famous was Temple Manor at Strood, Kent, for the purpose of lodging dignitaries traveling along Watling Street between London and Dover. The Temples famously held lands in Warwickshire, and Stowe.

There is a tradition which purports that shortly after the Crucifixion (63 A.D.), Joseph of Arimathea, Mary's uncle, was sent by the apostle Philip from Gaul to Glastonbury. King Arvirargus, son of Cynfelyn (Shakespeare's *Cymbeline,* reigned A.D. 9-40), granted him and his fellow missionaries 1440 acres of land (12 x 120) upon which to live and build a church.

This tradition is supported by the second century writings of Tertullian and Origen, as well as those of St. Gildas in the sixth century, who wrote that Britain was first illuminated by the light of "Christ the true Sun" in the reign of Tiberius Caesar. William of Malmesbury, who studied at Glastonbury in the twelfth century, also believed that these traditions were true. The great church councils of the middle ages always deferred to English bishops because of their claim to represent the earliest foundation of Christianity. It was only after the Reformation, when the Puritans turned against the old tradition, that apostolic origins of the English church were called into question.

In the secular world, it may have been that Joseph was involved in the tin mining business in southern England, which afforded him enough wealth and prominence in Palestine to hold a seat on the Sanhedrin.

We will begin with the tradition of Joseph and follow it as far as we can along the line of the Temples. The numbers at left refer to the number of generations each person was from Adam and Eve.

Continued from the Gospel of Matthew chart, page 45	...continued	
54 Rhesa	80 Frea (m. Woden!)	b. 219
55 Johanna	81 **Balder** (m. Nanna)	243-330
56 Judah	82 Brand	271-362
57 Joseph	83 Frithogar of Saxony	299-390
58 Shimei	84 Freawine	327-418
59 Mattathias	85 Wig(ger)	355-446
60 Mahath	(m. Thrytho)	
61 Naggai	86 Giwis	405-463
62 Hesli	87 Esla	411-502
63 Nahum	88 Elesa	439-558
64 Amos	89 King Cerdic of Wessex	467-534
65 Mattathias	90 King Cynric	495-560
66 Joseph	91 King Ceolin	550-593
67 Jannai	92 King Cuthwine	565-645
68 Melchi	Son of Ceawlin	
69 Levi	93 King Cutha(-wulf)	592-648
70 Matthat	94 Ceowald not king	622-88
71 Joseph of Arimathea	95 King Cenred	644-694
(brother of Mary's father Heli)	96 Ingild	680-718
72 Anna, his daughter	97 Eoppa	706-781
73 Penardim, her daughter	98 Eafa	732-762
(m. Llyr Ledaiath "King Lear")	99 King Alemund of Kent	758 788
74 King Bran of Siluria 40 BC-36 AD	100 Ecgbyht	771-839
75 King Caradoc of Siluria 8-80	101 King Ethelwulf	d. 857
76 King Cyllin of Siluria 40-125	(m. Osburga; Judith)	
77 Prince Coel 80-170	102 King Alfred Great	r. 849-901
78 Lleuver Mawr 137-181	103 Lady Ethelfreda	
79 Gladys* (m. Cadvan of Cambria)	104 Lady Elfwina	
	105 Leofwine	d. 1023

* Author's Note: Gladys' sister Eurgen married Aminadab. Their ancestors include Frothmund (84), Faramund (85), Clovis I (89), Charlemagne (98), and William the Conqueror (109).

106 **Leofric III**, K. of Leicester	978-1057	119 Thomas de Temple	1418-1500
m. **Lady Godiva**		m. Mary Gadney	
107 Algar, III, King of East Sxns		120 William Temple	1443-1532
m. Elgifu	d. 1062	m. Isabel Everton	
108 Edwin de Temple, Earl of East Saxons		121 Thomas Temple	1490-1560
m. Iwerydd Seisyll	1036-1071	m. Alice Heritage	
109 Baron Henry de Temple		122 Peter Temple	1516-1577
	1070-1095	m. Mylycent Jekyll	
110 Geoffrey de Temple		123 Sir John Temple	1542-1603
	1095~	m. Susanna Spencer	
111 John de Temple	1128-	124 Peter Temple	1576-1657
112 Henry de Temple	1164-	m. Katherine Kendall	
m. Lady Maud Ribbesford		(Brother of ~ Sir Alexander, MP ~)	
113 Baron Henry de Temple	1197-1250	(Brother of Elizabeth Fiennes)	
m. Lady Matilda		**125 Abraham Temple**	1597-1639
114 Baron Richard de Temple	1231-1295	m. Abigail Margaret Gifford	
m. Catherine de Langley		+ son John Temple	b. 1621
115 Nicholas de Temple	1265-1322		
m. Lady Margaret Corbet		* * * * * * * * * * *	
116 Richard de Temple	~1295-1346		
m. Lady Agnes de Stanley		126 Richard Templar	1623-1669
117 Nicholas de Temple	1335-1414	m. Joanna Shipley	
m. Maud of Burguillon		**127 Hannah Templar**	1643-1674
118 Richard de Temple	1379-1484	m. **Alexander Stewart**	
m. Joan Shepey			

See freepages.rootsweb.com/~shirlwbb/genealogy/TemplesofStoweexerpt.htm

18

Balder

243-330

How many of you have had a hard time getting out from under the shadow of your parents? I am sure it has happened to everyone, but none of you has had it as bad as I have. When your father is Woden and your mother is Frea (Frigg), you live in their shadow every Wednesday of your life; every Friday, too!

Not only that; they were gods. To add insult to injury, they gave my half-brothers Tiw and Thor their own days, Tuesday and Thursday. All I got was "Balderdash."

Just kidding. In Anglo-Saxon, my name *Baeldaeg* means "Day," so I had the last laugh – on all of them – every day was named ____-day! In the end, I got my own "day," but it was only after my death that they gave it to me.

You see, I was a rare breed of human – born without color in my flesh or in my hair. More than that, a strange light emanated from my forehead, making people think that I was a shining god! When I died (they weren't able to resurrect me), they named the first day of the week Sunday. They named the next day Monday after my wife, Nanna, a "moon" who took her light from me.

What about Saturday? That is a story in itself.

His name was Araknis, a dark-haired man who came from the Asir region of the Red Sea. Some people thought he was a wizard; others said that his father was a *Jinn* (a "Genie" – I am sure you have read about them). He wore a strange assortment of weeds (or magical herbs) in a ring around his head, which led the Norsemen to give him the nickname "Saturn." It was this "Saturn" who gave his name to Saturday.

When Araknis came up from the Red Sea, he brought with him a woman named Jordy, though she was not his wife. My father got on with her for a while, which made my mother exceedingly angry. Then Jordy was Thor's mother. We never knew who Tiw's mother was. He just showed up one day, in a basket.

In the Shadow of My Father

My father's name was Woden. He was born in Baktria, but he felt that he could do more with his life than simply herding sheep. He had a gnawing ambition: he wanted to become a god.

It is never easy for a man to become a god, so old Woden had to devise a plan. He studied a lot of gods and came up with a plan; a very good plan, at that.

The first thing a god needs is a group of worshipers. That is why he came to Norway. The people up here were a bit dense and would believe almost anything. (They called him a "shape-shifter," for he had shifted his outward habitat from the Middle East to the Far North... a change of "shape.") Then he needed to develop a reputation. This he did with the help of my mother, Frigg (every good god needs a worthy woman to boost his reputation). She was a spinner, first and foremost a spinner of wool, but she also knew how to spin a yarn. She told the Norsemen how my father had slain a *wyrm* (that is what they called a dragon). She told them that he had given up the sight in one eye in exchange for receiving wisdom, high up on a mountain (in fact he had lost it while riding a horse under a thicket), and to prove it my father invented *runes*, a system of writing (they looked more like chicken scratches to me). She convinced them that my father was a god of war (he was actually more adept at poetry), but they were disappointed when he never participated in war himself; he merely wrapped up their sprained ankles and said that he had healed them. His crowning achievement of "godhood" came when the Norsemen tested him by hanging him from their holy tree, Yggdrasil, to see what would happen. The only thing that happened was that his beard grew longer.

I guess he passed their test, for after that the Norsemen regarded my father as a god. That made me a little god; my half-brothers Thor and Tiw, too.

In the Light of My Mother

When my mother first saw me, she was worried about my safety, because, as I have said, I had no color in my skin. She thought this would make me so frail that anything could kill me. Being something of a sorceress in her own right, she decided to do something about it.

She concocted a special liquor* of toad skin, turnip, black mustard seed, holly, hound's tongue, a blind adder's sting, ivy, henbane, the resin of certain trees, tarragon, wolf's bane, root of hemlock, St John's Wort, the bark of a yew tree, foxglove, and a drop of her own blood, pricked from the spindle of her distaff.

She dressed in her robe of falcon wings, then pronounced the following incantation:

> "Vintery, mintery, cutlery, corn,
> Apple seed and briar thorn,
> Buttercups and Tartar's lips,
> Silvered in the moon's eclipse;

* Author's Note: Shakespeare's *Macbeth* opens with these, recited by the weird sisters.

Wire, briar, limber lock,

Three ravens in a flock;

One flew east, one flew west,

One flew over the eagle's nest.

Should any born of earth or air,

Yea, mineral, metal, animal, dare

To harm this child, the gods forsake –

His bones and sinews I shall unmake!"

Her *seider* finished, my mother rubbed the potion all over my body, taking care not to get any into my mouth, for it was highly poisonous. After that, I became invincible!

Through the Valley of the Shadow

My brothers and I couldn't pronounce the name *Araknis* very well, so we took to calling him by a nickname: "Loch Ness" (yes, we knew about Loch Ness long before the Vikings ever raided Lindisfarne: my mother grew up in Wales, not close, but on one of the British islands). We would shorten that to "Lochie" (spelled *Loki* in our language), or "Nessie," for sometimes he dressed like a woman.

Loki had a wife (not Jordy) that he brought with him from Asir, but if she took off her face cover, she looked like a camel. It was little wonder, then, that he began to look around Asgard to try to find a nicer looking woman. That is when the trouble began – he had eyes for *my* wife Nanna.

One night while my father was tasting the Mead of Poetry in his hall, Loki went to my mother, dressed as Nessie. He spoke words of licorice to her, trying to sway her.

"Tell me Balder's weakness," he implored her, "that I may be kind unto him."

Thinking it such a nice gesture that someone would be kind to her son, she told him.

"In my haste to enchant his pale skin," she confessed, "I failed to include one that grows not out of the earth, nor out of the air."

"I see," said the shapeshifter, (he too had come from afar). "And what of his wife, Nanna?"

"She is true to his body, and true to his soul," she confessed. "Why do you take such interest in Balder's wife?"

"Should misfortune befall him, what course would she take?" the Trickster asked her.

At that point, the veil was lifted from Frigg's eyes, and she knew what Araknis was up to. Then she refused to speak any further, but the damage was done.

I had a twin "brother" named Hodor (exactly the same age as me), another person that Araknis had brought with him from the Red Sea. While I had no trace of color in my flesh, Hodor had traces of every color, not only in his flesh, but in his hair; he was the son of Night and Other.

When we fought side by side, the one pure white, the other pure black, the enemy would often be so scared that they would turn around and run the other way or turn to fight someone else. Not only that, but Hodor refused to wear any armor, saying that if I wore none it was only honorable for him not to wear any. I guess he didn't really believe the effectiveness of the charm that my mother placed on me.

He got into a fix during a battle with a force of invading Romans. Though black and white were we, Hodor was not endowed with the lion's share of gray matter, so in the heat of battle, he turned to me to remark on the silly uniforms the Roman soldiers wore. Poor Hodor took an arrow in his chest and thought he was a goner, so instead of getting hacked up by those barbarians, he decided to end it all himself. Lying there on the ground, he took out his bow, tried to find his zenith, and shot his arrow straight up in the air. Then he lay his head down sideways on the ground, hoping the arrow would find his temple and put him out of his misery. He barely missed.

After the battle was over, we found Hodor lying there with one arrow in his chest and another in his head, but he was still alive. My brothers and I carted him back to Asgard, but we soon realized that he needed true medical attention, not the witch's brew that my mother would give him. We decided to take him down south to Midgard, where there was a hospital.

The "hospital" turned out to be a Norseman's hut, but it was well-equipped with all the herbs and tools a surgeon of the day needed: saws, drills, and Witch Hazel potion. It was found that the arrow in Hodor's chest had missed all his vital organs, so he would not die. Hodor's own arrow to the head had also missed its target (his brain), but it took out his optical nerve, blinding him.*

The Norseman nursed Hodor back to health. After a year or so, he returned to Asgard with three wood nymphs and a dwarf.

Frigg Sees and Describes My Death

Then one night I had a dream, the scariest dream I had ever had in my life. I dreamed that I was sinking – down, down, down I went, down the escarpment from Asgard to the fjord – and then I kept sinking, down, down, down under the water. I then realized that I was dead.

I went to tell my mother this dream. When I had finished, she looked troubled. Then she regarded me somberly and said, "I had the same dream, my son. I dreamt that you were sinking – down, down, down you went, down the escarpment from Asgard to the fjord – and then you kept sinking, down, down, down under the water. I then realized that you were dead."

Neither of us knew what to make of this dream, but it did not bode well for us. It was too bad to be true.

*Author's Note: This story combines the true stories of Herman Lehmann, a German immigrant kidnapped by Indians in Texas, who tried to end it all with a bow and arrow, and Harvey Stewart, who was blinded by a self-inflicted gunshot wound.

Shortly thereafter we were doing our *thing*, which was a kind of town meeting, a custom of the Norsemen. We played a game similar to "Blind Man's Buff." Since Hodor was blind, everyone put on a blindfold to level the playing field. I was invincible, so I stood in the middle of the circle and let them practice hurling their weapons at me. Most of the Norsemen fought with battle-axes, though some preferred bows and arrows. Thor used a sledgehammer. None could touch me.

Now Hodor had gotten a sword named "Mistletoe" from that dwarf who came back with him from Midgard. The nymphs had fashioned a special waistband from the leaves of the forest, and Loki prepared a magic potion to rub on his forehead. When it came time for Hodor to thrust his weapon at me, Loki uttered an incantation in his ear, enabling him to know exactly where I stood. His sword found its mark, and I, stunned, fell to my knees, mortally wounded. Everyone's jaw dropped. I had been killed!

Woden rode off on his horse Sleipnir to his summer home by a lake, just outside of Uppsala. From there he took a ship down south across the sea to a town called Hel. There he awoke a volvesse who had been sleeping for twenty years and asked her how to bring me back from the dead. She said that if every creature on earth, either alive or dead, would mourn me, she would invoke an ancient law that would return my breath unto me.

Araknis put on high boots and became Nessie, a giantess. Though all creatures great and small wept for me, their bright-eyed god, this oversized Nessie refused to mourn. I was thus condemned to eternal darkness. Fie on him (her?)!

The Norsemen prepared my ship, Ringhorn, with kindling and timbers. I boarded willingly, as did my grieving wife Nanna, and also the dwarf who had supplied that dreadful sword.

Torch lit timber, and off we sailed into the sunset.

19
Lady Godiva
~1080-1167

Perhaps you have heard of my wife, Godgyfu (you would know her as Lady Godiva.) She's the one who took that famous ride, a ride that rivals (if not betters) the Midnight Ride of Paul Revere and the Charge of the Light Brigade. The trouble is, she took her ride in broad daylight. Oh well, more about her later.

The First Vision

As I lay on my couch, of a sudden the walls of my bedchamber fell away. The garden was very dark green, with fragrant datura blossoms hanging down. I heard the sound of rushing water; I was drawn to it. Then I saw a bridge over a raging river. I joined a procession to the other side, but the bridge became a rope, all straight and narrow. Men crossing before me and behind me fell into the terrible river, their souls devoured by the teeth and tentacles of monsters. I balanced myself with a pole: on the left was the Lust of the Eyes; on the right, the Lust of the Flesh. The pole turned into a serpent named Pride of Life, so I cast it into the river and advanced to the other side. There, on a bright green lawn, people dressed in white gowns strolled about singing hymns. My dear departed mother Alwara threw her arms around my neck and greeted me: "Hello, Leafy." That was the pet name she used to call me as a child.

Leofric

My name is Leofric, son of Leofwine. I made my fortune in the mutton trade, out in Shropshire, and by some miracle my father and I survived the onslaught of Cnut at the battle of Ashington. Later on, King Cnut was angry at the Earl of Mercia, and killed him along with my brother. Lucky me. Cnut took a liking to me and made me Earl instead. When Cnut died, his son took over. That's when the tax collectors started ravaging the people of Mercia. Luckily, that king didn't last long. His half-brother Edward (the Confessor) took over. I had helped, so I was called the King-Maker.

The Second Vision

As I lay sleeping on my divan, I saw myself all dressed in white, wearing a shining green mantle. A beggar appeared at my door and presented me a ring. Its stone was red, though on closer inspection I realized that it was a crystal sphere containing a dram of blood. Its setting was some unknown metal, and the sphere was compassed about by twenty-three clusters of four jewels in the shape of X's – they all shone silver; plus one group in the shape of a Y shone gold. I went out of the chapel and saw the same beggar, who was John the Baptist. I returned the ring to his finger, whence he said, "The Water of Life."

The Countess of Leicester

I count it my utmost honor and blessing to marry Godgyfu, Countess of Leicester. She was heiress of an old Saxon family – related to the Sheriff of Lincolnshire. Her lands together with my fortune made us a very formidable couple. We dedicated our fortunes to the Church, building monasteries and nunneries in Worcester, Evesham, Chester, Leominster, Hereford, Wenlock, Stow-in-Lindsey, and of course, Coventry. She was also a patron of the arts.

The Third Vision

As I lay dreaming on my sofa, a loud noise such as the beating of many hooves came rumbling from the distance, until it thundered at my chamber door. Then saw I the angel Gabriel descending in a shaft of light. The light became so bright that I could no longer see the apparition, and I knew that it was God. "Behold I stand at the door and knock," He said. In my dream I opened the door, but then the Horsemen of Normandy swarmed over the land.

Politics & Conquest

I was forever at odds with Godwin, Earl of Wessex. When he threatened to attack King Edward, I intervened, saying that many good knights would be lost on both sides, leaving England exposed to her enemies. In the end his son, Harold Godwinson, depleted his army at Stamford Bridge, then lost the Battle of Hastings and let the Normans conquer England. Those guys just couldn't do anything right! Sadly, he left my little granddaughter widowed.

It was a good thing that Godgyfu and I had given away so much land to establish convents and priories. When the Normans took over, they confiscated everyone else's land, but they left the religious properties untouched.

Leofric's Visions

The Fourth Vision

As I lay on my bed in the still of night, a white bird lit on my sill and spoke to me. I couldn't make out its words, for it spoke in a dialect as yet unknown in England. "It is sheep, not mutton," I protested. "Swine, not pork; ox, not beef." Then the bird removed me to the Abbey. I stood at the Altar with Edward, and we saw the face of Christ in the Holy Eucharist, so we broke bread together. Then came a mighty hand above the Cross, and touching our heads, blessed us. "I am the Lamb of God," a voice said in a dialect that I well understood.

The Ride

Now let's get back to my wife's little escapade. Godgyfu virtually owned the town of Coventry, where we lived, but King Harthacanute had pressed me to levy a tax on the people there. So I taxed them. I taxed them down to the very manure they used to grow their crops. Always a friend of the poor, lovely Godgyfu insisted that I repeal the taxes. Well, which is worse, the wrath of your king or the wrath of your wife? I chose the wrath of my king... but could it have been avoided?

The first thing I did was to tax her pictures. None of the peasants had any artwork, so they would not be affected. Then I told her that if she would ride a horse stark naked through the town, from our castle to the church, I would quit taxing the people altogether. (After all, the ancient Greeks thought that the human body, as God's handiwork, was considered art.) She agreed. Then she went from door to door, telling the townsfolk what she planned to do. She ordered them to bolt their doors and close their shutters and NOT to look! Then she found a horse that hadn't been shoed and began her ride.

One resident, a tailor named Tom, came to me to tell me what she had done: she had ridden the horse through the marketplace, barefoot and bareback, without saddle, blanket or bridle, but she herself was fully clothed!

I couldn't help but laugh out loud when I heard that story. The ladies of the court were always playing such word games, and this time the joke was on me! I laughed so hard that I actually fell off my chair and injured my wrist. There were supposed to have been no witnesses.

I kept my word and rewarded her efforts. The townspeople of Coventry would not be taxed again. (I had to let stand a tax on horses, for that was in place before we ever came to Coventry.)

As for Peeping Tom, he was not so lucky. I blinded him with white-hot coals, not for telling me the truth, but for his insolence, and for having lusted in his heart. He had hoped to see a lady riding stark-naked on an elegant horse through the town, but instead he saw an elegant lady riding through the town on a stark-naked horse!

The sweet irony of it all! Godgyfu finally got what she had been waiting for so long. She has been immortalized in art.

Lady Godiva

20

Abraham Bernard Temple

1597-1639

The rumor that I was a "stowaway" got started one night while we were drinking ale at Beadle's. You see, the Logic of the Pint combined the fact that I was born at Stowe with the idea that I was a "castaway," our ship having been blown off course on the way over here from England. Oh, well, I guess I'll never live that one down. But let me tell you the real story.

Don't get me wrong: I was a devout Puritan, a *bona fide* member of the church. That didn't mean we were teetotalers. What was so "Puritan," about me, then? Good King Henry VIII had broken from the Italian Church, but everyone thought our English Church still needed some reforms. I was among them. We were tired of the elaborate rituals, decorations, and hierarchy of the Anglican Church. We just wanted to simplify things.

King James had put the Catholics to shame. He assembled three teams of translators, one at Oxford, another at Cambridge, and a third at Westminster. Each team translated the entire Bible into English, then they compared the results. It was a thing of beauty. Our family had one of the first copies printed.

We Temples go way back. My great-grandfather Peter was a Catholic, so Mary Queen of Scots bequeathed him land and a house in Buckingham. He no longer had to rent land in Warwick to raise sheep. To his good fortune, Parliament passed the "woolen cap law," which required all the commoners to wear a woolen cap to church on Sundays. This put money in his pockets. In fact, Great-Grandad Peter became the richest man in all of England, in his time.

It is said that great wealth dissipates quickly; by the second generation two-thirds are gone, and by the third generation... well, this is what happened to us. My grandad, Sir John, had twelve children. My father, Peter, also had twelve, but he was not well mentally (can you blame him, with all those mouths to feed?). In 1619 he was certified, and his meager inheritance was all but used up by my eleven brothers and sisters.

In those days the oldest brother would inherit his father's land; the second oldest would take up a profession, such as a lawyer; the third (or fourth, or fifth) would learn a trade. Since our family was involved in the wool trade, I took up tailoring.

Then Charles became king and launched a war with Spain. We still had to send wool to Belgium, because England was lagging behind in its ability to weave wool into finished cloth. When Charles got into it with Belgium, it squeezed off our source of revenue.

Luckily, I had some influential uncles. Sir Alexander had gained a seat in Parliament (until Charles dissolved it, that is), and my Aunt Elizabeth married William Fiennes, the Earl of Saye and Sele. William encouraged me to go to Connecticut, where he was trying to start a colony. Things were looking so depressed in England that I decided to take him up on his offer.

In 1631 I took my wife Abigail and our two sons Richard and Thomas (who were 8 years old and 6 years old, respectively) down to Bristol. There we boarded the good ship *White Angel* and sailed for my uncle's colony in Connecticut. As we neared the coast, however, a gale blew us off course; we finally landed safely in Saco, Mein.

The year that we first arrived in Mein, a company of thirty or forty bears (which are never mankind, i.e. fierce) went to the town of Gorgeana and killed fourscore settlers there. Wolves also marched in companies of ten or twenty, and seldom were they killed with guns or traps, but they preyed upon our cattle. First they killed the beast, then they returned at about midnight for their wolfish feast. What had we gotten ourselves into?

We stayed in Mein for about a year. Nobody needed any tailoring done, so I had to work as a mechanic in a mill. I saved enough money to travel, after a year's hard labor, and we finally moved south, settling in Salem. There were more people there, civilized people, so I set up my tailoring business with what little money I had saved from working in that mill.

I have a confession to make. I kept a wench named Maggie out in Concord. She had a son named Tobias, who was born before I ever came to the Colonies, but I raised him as though he were my own. Her other son Robert *was* mine. I hear she married John Gifford after I ... well, after I could no longer keep her.

*Author's Note: Some Internet sites claim that Abraham Temple is buried in the Old Hill Burying Ground (#279), Concord, Massachusetts. This epitaph reads, "Here lyes buried ye body of Mr. Abraham Temple who died Janry 4th 1738 aged 86 years & 7 months." This is Abraham B. Temple's (d. 1639) grandson.

As far as his son is concerned, Wyman's *Genealogies* (p. 937) lists two distinct personages, Richard Templar and Richard Temple, both of Massachusetts Bay Colony. The former is the father of Hannah Stewart (see #21, below); he moved from Yarmouth to Charlestown. The latter is the son of Abraham Temple; he moved from Salem to Concord. Most Internet sites confuse these two.

21

Hannah Templar Stewart
1643-1674

People used to joke that I was born in a barn, but that is only half-way true. I was born in Barnstable, Plymouth Colony, in the Year of Our Lord sixteen hundred and forty-three. Actually, I was raised as a young lady, according to the practices of our church.

My grandparents' families, including my father and mother, knew each other in Holland, where they went to escape the silly rules of the English Church. Life in Holland was peaceful, but it wasn't *English*, so they came here, where they could live as true English Christians. Grandpa Pritchard came to this rock in 1620, aboard the *Abigaile*.*

As little children, we were taught to be humble and submissive. As you know, children are born with a sinful nature and must be broken of our bad habits. We were not allowed to sit at the dinner table with our parents – we had to eat while standing. And no talking!

Charlestown

When I was four or five [1647] we moved to Charlestown, in Massachusetts. My father took a job in Mr. Willoughby's shipyard there. We purchased some land near Mr. [George] Bunker's hill. As a girl, I worked in the fields, cooked, fetched water, took care of the animals, and watched over the younger children. I also learned to sew, knead bread, and bake muffins. Sometimes I played games with the other children. I especially liked *gliffes*, which were tongue twisters, like "Dick the dog drunk drink in a dish."

In Charlestown I went to a "dame school" taught by Widow Tufts. Once a week I had to bring a log to burn in the fireplace, to pay her for her service. That log was heavy, and very hard to carry. Widow Tufts was a very strict teacher. If we turned around to talk, she would call us nasty names and belittle us. Maybe that is why we did what we did.

One time a strange multitude of caterpillars appeared in New England. We filled the pockets of our colorful skirts* with those itchy creatures and made up some excuse to go talk to Widow Tufts in the front. Then we released them behind the books that were on her desk. Can you imagine the Biddy's "surprised" reaction when that strange multitude emerged from behind the books?**

---

* Black dye was expensive, hence only the wealthy Puritans (who came to Massachusetts) wore it. Poorer Separatists who came to Plymouth wore blue, green, and orange.

Signs and Wonders

When I was nineteen, I married Alexander Stewart, a Scotsman that my father knew. My parents thought he was a good man, and he was not a Catholic, so everything seemed to be in accordance with God's will.

In 1664, a great comet appeared over New England for three months. We took this as a sign. Indeed it was, for in that year the Dutch Colony of New Amsterdam was captured by England.

A Great Fire

Just about the time that little John was born [1667], we heard some terrifying news: the town of London had burned. Though people thought it was started by foreigners or Catholics, they found out that a cow had tipped over a lantern and burned its own barn, itself included. People in Charlestown say that it was God's way of venting his wrath on that gluttonous town, for the fire started on Pudding Lane and ended on Pye Corner.

I could never imagine living in a town as large as London. All my life I have lived here in the colonies, first in Plymouth, then in Massachusetts. There are only about a hundred and fifty houses here…one thousand people, in all; not counting the Indians, that is.

I had been to Boston once, when we moved from Yarmouth. It was the last stop before crossing the river into Charlestown. Later that town had its own fire, but I'm sure it didn't compare to the one in London-town.

Mother Goose

Just after our Samuel was born [1669], little Eliza Foster came to live with us. Her father, captain of a ship named *Dolphin*, was captured (along with Eliza's brother) by Turks while transporting a load of fish to Bilbao, Spain. The Prince of Turks vowed never to release his captive slaves as long as he should live. Mr. [Increase] Mather said that we should pray earnestly to God, and that we did. Within two years the Turkish prince was killed in a war, and Mr. Foster was delivered back unto us, alive and well.

Little Eliza had quite a way with words. She was good at *gliffes*, and always making up rhymes. For example, "Old widow Gretchen, asleep on her dais; the swine in her kitchen, the kine in her maize." Or,

** This fictional episode reflects the true story of this author's mischief during his sophomore year of high school, when he released a lab rat behind the books on Mrs. Clegg's desk.

Hillary dillary doll,
The mouse ran up the wall.
The cat said, "Please,"
The mouse ate cheese.
Hillary dillary doll.

I heard that Eliza grew up and had so many children she didn't know what to do. She married old Mister Vergoose and became known as "Mother Goose."

Our daughter Margaret is our fifth child, born in August [1674]. She's adorable, but these two weeks have been really hard for me. I continue to bleed, and the pain will not cease. Oh, how I wish Deacon Fuller were still with us…*

* Author's Note: Hannah died August 21, 1674, nineteen days after Margaret was born.

22

Pietro Alberti *
1608-1655

Alberti

My father was Andrea Alberti, Secretary of the Ducal Treasury of Venice. My mother was Lady Veronica Cremona, a daughter of the de Medici family. We were Florentine merchants and long-time treasurers of the Pope. Our fortunes had soured miserably due to the Black Death, which reduced the population of Venice by 60%. But that was not exactly why I left.

In our house were many mansions, but in each nook and cranny lurked a multitude of evil, intrigues as befits the basest nature of Man. Perhaps that is why I was lured to the teachings of John Calvin. As Augustine had written about original sin, I felt that man cannot save himself; he needs divine help. I observed the people around me and concluded that only a few could have been chosen by God; the others were probably fated to burn. For the chosen few, Christ shed his blood on the cross: God's irresistible grace will flow upon them like a flood. To this end, the saints must persevere.

The English were always playing word games. Just as the Greeks had devised the "ICHTHUS" logo,** the Brutes called Calvin's teachings "TULIP" – Total, Unconditional, Limited, Irresistible, Persevering. Maybe that is why I went to Holland. My own family were staunch Catholics, and I had to make a choice: either abandon my beliefs or abandon my family (and face the consequences…the de Medicis were most unforgiving). Sadly, I chose the latter. I went to Holland and joined the Dutch Reformed Evangelical Church.

* Pietro Cesare Alberti is renowned in New York City for being the first Italian immigrant to the New World. Pietro's granddaughter Isabel married Hannah and Alexander's son John Stewart.

** ICHTHUS = "Jesus Christ Son of God, Savior."

I then sailed on the good ship *De Coninch David* ("King David") as a crew member, but I fought with the captain the whole way. He threatened to throw me off at Cayenne, but I managed to stay on. When we got to New Amsterdam, I had to sue him for my wages. I was lucky to get anything.

Mr. Montfoort was good enough to let me use a portion of his land out on Long Island to grow tobacco. In 1639, I built a mansion and tobacco plantation at Wallabout.

In 1642 I married Judith Manje, whose parents (Jan and Martha) were Dutch (I was the only Italian in New Amsterdam, so this was a good choice). Her parents gave us a nice house on the Canal to call home.

By 1647 I had a hundred acres on Long Island, so we gave up our house on Broad Street and moved out there with our two children (1646). Four other children were born after that.

One fine day Judith and I were out working in the fields. Wait! What's that noise? Darned savages! I told the housekeepers to make sure the children were well hidden away in the cellar…

Pietro C. Alberti

From NY to TX

Hello, Everybody.

Thank you all for coming. Now I would like to say a few words to my son. Though we ate dinner and watched TV together nearly every night, we never really talked. There are some things that must be said that were never said, so I will say them now, in front of everyone.

One day last year, in June of 2016, I was waiting at a red light down there by that futon store near the corner (Kawamura Futon). They had some of those bothersome flags outside, the kind that businesses put out on the sidewalk to attract customers. Stopped by the red light I had time to read them, so I did. They announced the 450th anniversary of the futon store. It was established in 1666, the same year as the London fire.

So I got to thinking, you and I are Americans living in Japan, but not many people can appreciate the import of that. I'm sure you have asked yourself these questions, as we all have: Who am I? Where do I come from? Where am I going? When will I get there? If you will indulge me, I will attempt to answer some of those questions for you.

I am Jan E.J. Stewart, and I was born in Los Angeles. My father was Leonard Jackson Stewart, who was born and raised in Texas. His father was Alva Clinton Stewart, and I'll side-step a bit to talk about his wife (my grandmother), who was born Minnie Evelyn Passmore. Now her father was Leonard Jackson Passmore, and *her* mother was Rachel Eliza Banta.

Rachel's father was John Banta, who was born in Indiana. His father Isaac moved the family to Texas in 1839. Isaac's father David Banta was born in Kentucky, and his father, Hendrick Banta III, was born in New Jersey. Where there is a third, there must be a second, and of course, a first. Hendrick the First's father was Jacob Epke, who was born in Holland in 1616.

Now this Jacob Epke is a person of interest, because in 1659 he sold his windmill (I'm not joking – he really had one) and booked passage on the good ship *De Trouw* ("Faith") for the New World. He purchased land from Peter Stuyvesant in New Amsterdam, which was captured five years later by the British, who changed its name to New York. That was in 1664, so I guess we've got the futon shop beat by about two years, or seven years, depending on how you look at it.

Well, I'll bring my little history lesson to a close with the words of a song by Susan Werther:

"There is a hope
That's been expressed in you
The hope of seven generations, maybe more.
And this is the faith
That they invest in you
It's that you'll do one better than was done before."

I hear that you are going to Barcelona next week, perhaps to find your roots. May I suggest that someday you go to New York, where your true roots lie. Today Jacob Epke's land is located on the southwest corner of Broad Street and Water Street, in the financial district. And just a stone's throw away is William Street. That place is like a magnet for us. Your mother and I ate breakfast there two summers ago in "This Little Piggy" [the Hanover] Deli. Earlier this year your sister Hillary and her family went to New York and stayed in the Hampton Hotel. She didn't know it, but the Hampton Hotel was built on that exact same piece of land that Jacob Epke bought from Peter Stuyvesant in 1659.

May I suggest that one day you "find yourself" by going back to that sacred piece of land in Manhattan, and possibly find your true calling, and strive to do one better than what went before.

And sometime in the future, perhaps twenty-five years from now, as you stand here at your own son's wedding ... [pause] ... please remember me.

... August 6, 2017

The Bantas

This surname has been traced from early times from Champagne, France. *Bant* was an island in Friesland, now known as a village north of Emmeloord in the Netherlands. (Friesland was the original home of the Saxons.) Spelling variations include Ban, Bans, and many more.

Lleuwe te Bonte (1540-   )
Epke (Luuesz) Luuesz (1569-1630)
(Jacob Epkeszn Te Bonta) (1591-1656)
Jacob Epke (1619-ca 1686/-90) #1 (p. 40)
Hendrick Banta I (1655-1717) #4 (p. 64)
Hendrick Banta II (1696-1740) #34 (p. 90)
Hendrick Banta III (1718-1805) #161 (p. 134)
David Hendrick Banta (1771-1841) #493 (p. 230)
Isaac William Banta (1800-1855) #1546 (p. 396)
John Walter Banta (1833-1914) #2758 (p. 670)
Rachel Eliza Banta (1874-1943) #4584 (p. 672)
Minnie Evelyn Passmore (1892-1973)
Leonard Jackson Stewart (1914-1988)
Jan E.J. Stewart (1948-   )

The hash mark (#) refers to each individual's number in the book, *A Frisian Family.*
Page numbers are given for readers' convenience.

23
Epke Jacobs
1619-1686

My name is Epicurus Jacobson (*Epke Jacobse*, in Dutch... that's because I was born in Holland). We Epicureans are all alike – gourmets with a capital G.

My grandfather, Epke Luuesz, and grandmother Coely Sil Cornelisda owned a farm called Jelargerma, a few miles northwest of Minnertsga, in Friesland. After my grandfather died, my grandmother bought more property from her sister and her husband.

My father Jacob Epkesz lived on a large farm at Arum. My mother was Reytske Sickedr.

When I grew up, I owned a windmill near Minnertsga. In 1652, when I married Sitske Dirckse, we bought a house in the village of Easter-bierum, but things didn't work out, so we sold it at a loss and returned to Minnertsga. All of our sons were born in Holland: Cornelius ('52), Seba ('54), Hendrick ('55), Dirck ('57) and Weart ('58).

I think it was baptism that got us into hot water with the authorities. You see, the state religion was the Reformed Protestant Church, but we practiced infant baptism. I baptized my eldest son Cornelius as "Egbert," more for acceptance by the locals than for purity of form. In 1656 I was arrested and fined for allowing a Roman Catholic priest into my house to baptise my son Hendrick. To me it didn't matter if he was reformed or Dutch reformed or Catholic. A priest was a priest. I just wanted to have my son baptized.

In October of 1657 there was such a bitter east wind, lasting for three days, that the water of the Zuyder Zee escaped in many places. You could walk from the island of Ens to Friesland, if you had a good reason (or if you lacked reason). Our farm was completely flooded. What followed was a fierce and long winter. We barely had enough to eat, let alone grain to sell to the neighbors.

Minnertsga

The winds had completely shredded the sails of my windmill, and most of the struts were damaged beyond repair. It would cost half a year's living to make it operational again. It was therefore a most difficult decision, but one that I discussed thoroughly with my family – and we decided to move to the New World.

The New World

I paid for passage on the good ship *De Trouw* ("The Faith"), 36 Florins for myself, 108 Florins for my wife and five sons, ages ¼, 2, 3, 4, and 6 years, as well as 15 Florins cash.

Upon arrival we bought a house on Manhattan Island. There we lived a happy life for a year and a half, until Sitske died. Then (1662) I decided to take the boys and move out to Vlissinger [Flushing], on the north shore of Long Island, about 12 miles from New Amsterdam.

Something happened in September 1664. Maybe it was a good thing; I don't know. Four English ships arrived and seized our colony. Their king, Charles II, had given all the land between the Delaware River and Connecticut River to his brother James, Duke of York, in exchange for four beaver pelts. (The nerve of them: they didn't even offer to repay the 60 guilders worth of trinkets that Mr. Minuit had used to buy the island from the Lenape Indians in the first place.) They renamed our colony New York.

I said it may have been a good thing. That is because Mr. Stuyvesant had been against religious freedom, giving the Dutch Reformed Church advantage over Lutherans, Quakers and Catholics. When the English navy arrived, Stuyvesant tore up their Articles of Capitulation, but his son pieced it back together and persuaded him to sign it. After that, we had religious freedom.

In 1671 I bought a new mill in the town of Jamaica, between Seller Neck (Old Town Neck) and Plunder Nek (Long Neck), but I sold it a few years later. In 1675, I moved with my sons to Bergen, across the river from New York, in what they called New Jersey. Then I purchased land in the New Plantation, on the Hackensack River. Finally, in 1686 I got 240 acres on Cherry Hill, Spring Valley. It measured 14 ½ chains by 170 chains.

* Author's Note: One chain equals 66 feet, or 1/10 of a furlong, or 1/80 of a mile. An acre is ten square chains.

That same year I had some trouble. Though we owned the land, Gawain Lawrie, the English governor, decreed that we would have to pay rent. We refused. The High Sheriffe of Bergen County brought me, my two youngest sons, and five others before the magistrate for refusing to obey the King's authority. We were committed to the Com'on Gaole of Woodbridge until we each one gave one hundred pounds [as bail] to guarantee our personal appearance at the Court, to be held April next. We were simply Dutch farmers, manfully standing up for what we deemed were our rights.

Epke Jacobse

Author's Note: Most of the information we can glean about these early pioneers comes from the records of land titles, that is, property which was sold to them or by them. This leaves a dearth of information about who they were and what they did, in other words, it leaves us guessing as to their actual lives. Little else is known about Hendrick I and II, other than their respective wives' names. Probably most influential was Hendrick III, who moved from Pennsylvania to Kentucky with twelve of his younger children, and who knows how many grandchildren. There are now 6515 people in the US with the family name Banta. They leave behind a street named after them in Hackensack, New Jersey. However, I will skip several generations and pick up again in Pennsylvania, with a grandson of Hendrick III, Isaac William Banta.

24
Isaac William Banta
1800-1855

They say life is a journey; mine was quite a trip. I started out in Lexington, Kentucky. From there I moved to Princeton, Indiana. That's where I met Eliza Barker. She said she was related to Queen Elizabeth, but I didn't care. As far as I was concerned, Eliza Barker was my queen. We got married in 1822.

We had thirteen children: Henry Wilson ('23), Mary Ann ('25), William Milton ('27), David Riley ('29), Celesteen ('31), **John Walter** ('33), Jacob Rhinerson ('35), Abia Louise ('37), Roxanna ('39), George Wilson ('41), Permelia Victory ('43), Elizabeth Perlina ('44), and Isaac Flavius Josephus ('48).

Sometimes I worked as a mechanic, sometimes as a carpenter. We had a good life going for us in Indiana, but sometimes you just get a yearning for something more.

"Many moons and many seasons have come and gone, and it is really an unknown factor which would enter into this puzzle of life that would introduce into the minds of two people the thought to uproot their whole family and their way of life to emigrate unto an untried, untested wilderness area that was burgeoning with many other similar nomads who had come to set up homesteads in this wild, untamed west, still populated and overrun by the barbaric ways of the savage Red Man."

… L.J. Stewart, *"Old" John Banta*

We just wanted to raise cattle. Eliza and I longed for the free and open range of Texas, where we could engage in cattle ranching on the luxurious grasses, which were at that time free to all. So in the autumn of 1839 we loaded our household goods into huge wagons, and with ox teams, set out for our new "home on the range."

We arrived with nine of our children in Clarksville, Red River County, some time late in the autumn of the following year. Here we stayed for some time, I followed my trade as carpenter, then the desire for the "frontier" became stronger, and we set out again, finally locating on what was known as Bullard Creek.

There we raised cattle.

25

John Walter Banta

1833-1914

My youth and teenage years were probably typical of any young man living on the frontier. I went to school in a one-room schoolhouse. When I wasn't hard at work on my father's farm, helping with the cattle, I enjoyed hunting and fishing.

I moved with my family to Hamilton's Valley (Burnet, Texas) between 1851 and 1854. During that time, I was introduced to the Christadelphian Church. My grandfather David, when he moved to Indiana, was unable to get a Dutch Reformed preacher, so his church disintegrated; the Dutch families joined other dominations in the neighborhood (New England laws dictated that if there was not a suitable church, people should join one nearby). Subsequently Grandad became a Baptist Minister. My brother David Riley became a Universalist preacher. The Christadelphians were about the same as the Universalists, so I joined the Christadelphians.

In 1855 the Grim Reaper paid us a visit, and my Dad went to await the grand coming to the Glory Land. Four years later my Mom married Mr. Zachariah McDonald and moved to a farm on the Pedernales River. I was 26 years old at the time, so I stayed on with my brother Henry in Burnet. My younger brother George went with Mom and her new husband to Fredericksburg.

Marriage and Family

I made quite a few visits to Mom and Zach. On one of those visits I made the acquaintance of a lovely Scotch* girl from the Doss Valley area. Her name was Rebecca Angelina McDonald, daughter of Thomas and Rachel McDonald. In 1860 I married her. All our children were born in Burnet: Mary Alice ('61), Isaac T ('62), William ('63), Clara ('65), Henry Wilson ('67), Martha Jane ('69), John Oscar ('70), Ira ('72), **Rachel** ('74), Epke Seth ('77), Oliver C ('78), and Lafayette.

* Author's Note: Rebecca Angelina McDonald traces her lineage through her grandfather Linville McDonald back to the Viking King Ivar II of Waterford, in Southern Ireland. Of her forefathers, five were born in the American colonies, twelve in Ireland, and ten in "Scotland" (that is, the Western Isles). Ivar himself was probably born in Ireland, as his grandfather lived there. John MacDonald (b. 1318) married Margaret Stewart, whose father was King Robert (II) Stewart. I suspect that the McDonalds moved to America (and changed their name) when they lost Dunnyveg Castle to the Campbells in 1615.

I Kill an Indian Chief

After the war, I joined the Texas Rangers… a captain, at that. One day we heard of an Indian raid nearby. It was a misty, rainy day. We could tell how many there were by looking at the dry spots where they had been sleeping. Eleven of them. As luck would have it, there were eleven of us… a virtual football game with eleven players each! But we would play this game for keeps.

We tracked them down. We were all on horseback, but they were on foot. Even so, they gave us a run for our money. At about four o'clock in the afternoon we caught up with them. I guess they figured they couldn't keep running, so they turned around to fight. And some fight it was.

The arrows were flying all around us. It was frustrating because we had old-style muzzle-loading flintlock rifles, which used Mexican powder and lead caps. For each shot we took, we had to stop, re-load, then fire again. The powder on a flintlock burns like a fuse for about five seconds, but when you are facing a barrage of Indian arrows, five seconds seems like an eternity. Luckily, we only had two casualties. One was an arrow that landed on the toe of my boot. (The other passed through a young Ranger's clothing but merely grazed his flesh.)

When the Indians turned around to retreat, I shot their chief from about 200 yards off. He fell to the ground, mortally wounded. I approached, meaning to scalp him, but he was still alive. Seeing me come near, and not wanting to be scalped, he drew a butcher knife from his belt and plunged it into his own breast. That was fine with me, for I didn't want to scalp a live Indian chief.

After the fight we assessed the damages. We counted five "good" ones ("The only *good* Indian is a *dead* Indian"). Then we looked around and counted three sets of tracks, which made eight. That meant that the three Indians who survived had probably carried off their wounded, one wounded per each healthy Indian. At any rate, there were at least five "good" Indians. The world would be a safer place.

In March 1898, Angeline and I moved to Verde Creek, in Kerr County. Camp Verde, a military camp, became famous when Jefferson Davis, President of the Confederacy, introduced the camel as a beast of burden to carry freight across the desert from California, through Arizona and New Mexico, to Texas. Horses and mules would wear their shoes down while walking across the sharp volcanic glass of the desert, but camels' feet would spread out softly, enabling them to traverse the same terrain easily. I never rode a camel; it was strictly horses for me.

Angie and I finally moved to a little town called Mason, on the Llano River. There were quite a few of our relatives living there, so we bought a little frame house on the highway. Here we would wait until our Lord and Savior calls forth to gather His flock into the fold on the day of resurrection.

Angeline and John Banta

26
Rachel Eliza Banta
1874-1943

In my teen years I went to school at Onion Creek, Texas. My teacher was P.G. Temple, a former Captain in the Civil War, so he was known as the "Old Captain."

Another student in the school was a young, good-looking boy with a quiet, charming manner about him, a devilish gleam in his dark brown eyes, and a ready chuckle from his sparkling good humor. His name was Leonard Passmore. We were childhood sweethearts. One day the Old Captain got hold of my autograph album and wrote these verses:

> "Miss Rachel, I admire
>   Your brilliant eyes;
> And therefore I desire,
>   That you be learned and wise.
>
> Don't let your heart go yearning,
>   A household drudge to be;
> Apply yourself to learning,
>   And as the air, be free.
>
> And when you've grown more stable,
>   And learn more of this state,
> Your judgement will be able
>   To choose a proper mate."

Leonard then "picked a crow" with the Old Captain for insinuating that he was not a "proper mate" for me, but the Old Captain said that he meant to tell me to go to school a little longer before getting married. Anyway, another fellow besides Leonard had his eye on me, too.

The Old Captain got hold of my album once more and wrote in that other fellow's section,

"Miss Rachel, I've been seeking
   A corner or a nook,
Within your heart; but failing,
   I steal within your book."

After reading that, I suspected that it was the Old Captain, not the other fellow, who really had a crush on me.

Graduation Day at the San Saba River

In the summer of '91 I went with my father, mother, sister and brother to Washington State to harvest hops. That wasn't the real reason we went. The real reason was that my father wanted me to get away for a while before I did something "foolish" (like get married). I was only seventeen, you see. My cousin "Tex" lived in Tacoma, and he offered his advice, which I thought was pretty good. He said, "It is easier to turn a 'no' into a 'yes' than it is to turn a 'yes' into a 'no'." I told him I would think hard on those things.

My brother didn't come back to Texas with us; he stayed on with Tex in the Olympic mountains to become a mountain man. I suppose it was their "manifest destiny."

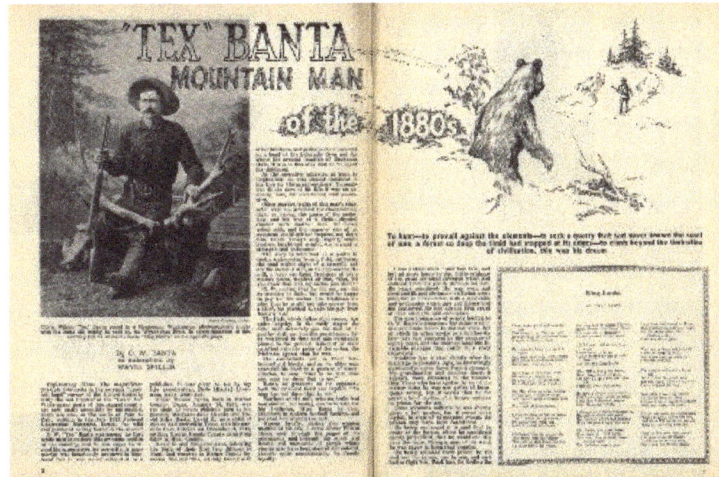

Ignoring my cousin's advice ("Let your yeas be yeas and your nays be nays"), in November of that year I married Leonard Passmore at Spring Creek (much to the Old Captain's chagrin). Come to the point, Leonard was a much better poet than the Old Captain. (He was much cuter, too!) We lost two children in infancy, but five girls and two boys survived.

Leonard taught in the same school we had attended at Onion Creek. (I don't know what the Old Captain thought about that!) We bought 20 acres of land from Leonard's father, and there we set up housekeeping. We later bought another hundred acres from his father, and with that we had a pretty good start in farming. Leonard's main occupation was teaching, however.

One of our children, Minnie, went on to marry Alva Stewart.

The Passmores

The name Passmore originated at a village called Peasemore (originally spelled Praxemere). It means "to pass or go across a moor," or possibly "a mer," in which case it referred to a seafarer. The first settler in the United States was Thomas Passmore, who landed in Virginia in 1624.

Thomas Passmore, 1598-1662
    m. Jane Paulk, 1603-1690
    George Passmore, ca 1651-1751
        m. Elizabeth Unk
    John Passmore 1720-1754
        m. Sarah Bailey
    Robert Passmore 1750-1785
        m. Mary Houseman
    Houseman Passmore 1773-1829
        m. Mary Unk
    John Passmore 1807-1872
        + Candacy (unmarried);
        m. Sarah Lee (spouse)
    Andrew Jackson Passmore 1831-1910
        m. Epsey Cato
    Leonard Jackson Passmore 1873-1936
        m. Rachel Eliza Banta
    Minnie Evelyn Passmore 1892-1973
        m. Alva Clinton Stewart

27

John Passmore
1807-1872

I was born in Georgia, a sixth-generation American. In those days we didn't keep track of our progenitors. I know my father Houseman married Mary, one of the Unk family girls. Word has it that my great-great-grandfather George married Elizabeth Unk, but I have no way of knowing whether she was related to Mary, my mother. The Passmores and the Unks had been long-time family friends. And a little bird tells me that *his* father, Thomas, married Jane Paulk in England. The two of them came to Jamestown while it was still a fledgling colony, then moved to Mary's Hundred, Maryland. As for me, I married Sarah Gilbert.

Though I was born in Washington County, it was Lincoln who caused all the commotion. After the war, the South was in a pitiful condition. Carpetbaggers came in droves, trying to make us change our way of thinking. Then they passed the Fourteenth. I didn't think things would ever be the same. I heard a lot of good things about Texas from some former Rangers who had fought with the Confederate Army, so me and Sarah decided it would be for the better if we headed out west.

After some deliberation, we packed all our household goods and victuals onto our oxcart and set out from Jacksonville. We took a horse for Sarah to ride on and a cow to give us milk during the trip. I packed my Yankee rifle, a .44 caliber Henry "Sixteener" – the rifle you could "load on Sunday and shoot for the rest of the week." There were still lots of Injuns out in Texas.*

The trip took a month, for it was over a thousand miles. We bought 200 acres from T.J. Smith and Charles Nimitz** and built a log cabin there. Our two boys Alexander and Bryan came with us.

* Author's Note: For those among you who refer to the Indian Removal Act (1830) as the "Trail of Tears," I invite you to read the firsthand accounts of some of the early pioneers of this country. Then count, on all your fingers and toes, the number of innocent settlers (men, women, or children) who were hacked to death or kidnapped by Indians. I would surmise that many of you cry-babies have ancestors (grandparents, perhaps great-grandparents) who only arrived on this continent after "the West was won," and have no concept of the hardships the pioneers suffered to make your lives here comfortable and prosperous.

** The father of WW II Admiral Chester Nimitz.

Bryan settled down in Gillespie County, down around the Pedernales River. Alex went up around Clyde.

One day my boy Alex was standing in front of the screen door of their home, holding baby Etta in his arms, when a shot rang out. He fell dead where he stood. We didn't know if it were Injuns or not… never did find out. Some of 'em had Winchesters, though.

28

Andrew Jackson Passmore
1831-1910

The Magnetic North of Man

When you fashion a sword in full wrath,
    It has no magnetic field;
When you temper the blade in its bath,
    Its polarity's once again sealed.

But if your blade faces not north
    When it's drawn from the water anew,
'T'will prove neither mettle nor worth,
    For it will not swing straight, nor true.

So the soul of each one of us proves,
    When drawn from its baptismal font,
Which direction its helmsman moves,
    If salvation is that which we want.

    Who shall guide us to the Promised Land?
    But Christ, the Magnetic North of Man!

You may glean from my little poem that I was a blacksmith by trade. That I was. I was also a devout Baptist (until we moved to Texas, that is).

By my name you can guess that I was related to Old Hickory. That much I claim as true, but I won't tell you exactly how.*

I was born in Georgia in the Year of Our Lord 1831. When I was 21 years of age, I met Epsey Cato. We were married within a year. Then we moved to Jacksonville, Florida.

* See footnote on following page.

Early in '63 I joined the Confederate Army: Florida 11th Infantry, Company D. (That there "infantry" is an odd word in itself... you would think they wanted little children to do their fighting. The word comes from the Latin *infans*, meaning newborn, foolish, or speechless. That was about it... we didn't have any say in what we were told to do.) I took with me a 3x5 inch Bible and a small Spanish dirk, in case I needed them. I needed the Bible. As it turned out I didn't have much use for the dirk.

The officers had promised me that I could go home to be with Epsey when it came time for her to deliver the baby, but when that time came, they double-crossed me. That's why I deserted. The twits were not men of honor. (I wanted to use my dagger on them, but I didn't.) Once I got home, I had to hide out in the attic to avoid the sentries they placed in front of our house. After l'il Andrew was born in the summer of '63, I gave up and went back to the war.

Things were going along all right until the spring of '64, when we went up to Petersburg. They called it a "siege," but it was more of a long, drawn-out attack. Our unit got cut off from the others, and we were captured! Drat! (Actually, this probably saved my life. A year later our entire company surrendered at Appomattox – we had started out with over a hundred, but only four officers and nineteen men remained.) The Yanks planned to march us up to Pennsylvania from Virginia.

* Author's Note: Leonard.J. Stewart (my father), in his "Biographical Sketch," writes that many of AJP's offspring swore up and down that he was the son of Old Hickory. (Pres. Andrew Jackson had no legitimate offspring – his only children were a nephew and a Creek Indian, both of whom he adopted.) AJP had a half-brother, Alexander, who was about the same age, presumably the son of Sarah Lee ("Nobody doesn't like Sarah Lee"). This implies that AJP was the son of his father's mistress Candacy. Both brothers were legitimized in 1852 by an act of the Georgia Legislature. If Candacy had been involved with Old Hickory at some point, well, who knows? We don't know what Candacy looked like, or Sarah Lee, for that matter. However, LJS repeatedly refers to AJP as "a red-haired, blue-eyed Irishman." Red hair is a characteristic trait of Scotsmen, not Irishmen (except perhaps those Scots who migrated to Ulster Plantation in the 1600s). Old Hickory's father immigrated to the U.S. from Ireland. Our "two plus two" here illustrates fuzzy math at best; whether AJP descended from Ireland's Hugh Jackson or from Jamestown's Thomas Passmore is not clear.

It seems that William of Normandy (the Conqueror, 1066) was not the only royal to base his claim to the Throne on a night in the hay!

We thought it strange that they should make us stand guard over ourselves at night, but there was probably no place a runaway soldier dressed in a Rebel uniform could hide. One night my friend got sick, so I volunteered to do a double shift for him. I was getting a bit sick myself, so I fell asleep on guard duty. The Yanks made it clear that this was a capital offense; I would face the firing squad the following day.

Come sun-up, though, they said that Honest Abe (their commander-in-chief) had got wind of my plight and exonerated me. I doubted their story, but only a fool would argue against them. It was more likely that if they shot me, they would have to explain their behavior to their commanding officer, and he would find out that they were making us prisoners stand guard duty (which in fact was their responsibility), and *they* would be shot for dereliction of duty!

By the time we got to Philadelphia I had become so sick that they had to hospitalize me. I was grateful for that nurse who said, "This Confederate soldier is so malnourished!" She herself vowed to nurse me back to health. Maybe she was just struck by my blue eyes (she was Pennsylvania Dutch). I don't know.

I was discharged from the hospital, and discharged from the army, but the war was still raging, and I was stuck in Pennsylvania. I went to a local smithy and asked him for a job, but he said I was probably too weak even to work the bellows. He gave me a few bucks to help me on my way, an act of kindness that I will never forget (not to mention that kind nurse who fed me).

I went on down to New Jersey, where I got a job in a glass factory. When the war ended, I walked home. Yes, you heard that correctly. I walked home to Florida from New Jersey. It was nearly a thousand miles, so my dogs ached. (I hear that my granddaughter still has that Bible and dagger; I don't know for certain.)

Reconstruction

When the war started, the army confiscated everyone's horses, but they didn't want our old blind mule. Epsey needed to plow the fields by herself, so she broke two wild oxen to do the job.

While I was gone my neighbor stole that old blind mule from Epsey. After I returned I went over there, beat the neighbor up, and got our mule back. That'll learn him! You just don't rustle a mule from a nice little lady like Epsey.

A few years later, my Dad and Sarah pulled up their roots and moved to Texas! Of all places! Dad wrote back and told us how great things were out there, so Epsey and I did the same. It took a while, but we finally arrived in Onion Creek.

One thing I hated about Texas was the frogs. Horrid, squishy creatures! One time we were having a picnic, when some of the little kids went out and gathered a bunch of frogs in a bucket. The women needed a place to dispose of the chicken feathers, so they threw them into another bucket. Unbeknownst to them, the men had previously tossed some unused shells from our hunting trip into… a bucket! Then the ladies tossed their bucket of feathers onto the fire. All the men started scrambling to get out of there. "Are the frogs exploding?" I asked. "No," they shouted. "It ain't the frogs!"

Andrew Jackson Passmore

Epsey

29

Leonard J. Passmore

1873-1936

A Mexican Lynx

I guess I was about sixteen years of age when I killed that Mexican lynx. It was the large spotted kind, with tufts in its ears.

My father owned a great many hogs that were running loose on the ranges, and in order to pen them in we had to keep a large coterie of dogs. They were named Sport, Drive, Fannie and Beaver; in addition, someone had given me a pup. The dogs were wearied and footsore, so on that day my father let me take the pup out with old Beaver in order to let the other dogs rest.

I walked about two miles down Onion Creek when I heard Beaver and the pup barking furiously. I ran to the dogs and saw a large lynx up in a tall blackjack tree. I had no gun, and I knew that Beaver and the pup could not kill it, so I began to scream, hoping that a nearby farmer would hear me and bring a gun. No one came.

At last I fell upon the plan of tying my pocket-knife to the end of a pole and thrusting it at the lynx. I used my own shoe-strings to secure the knife to the pole and climbed up into the tree. As hard as I could strike, the knife did not penetrate the tough hide of the lynx, which jumped out of the tree. The dogs gave chase but the lynx, having just finished its lunch, was plum tuckered out and hid in a small live oak. I pelted it with rocks, and it ran away again to a small post-oak. I tried poking it with my knife, but the lynx snatched the knife in its mouth. I gave it a shove and drew blood, upon which the lynx ruined my shoe-strings and chewed the wooden handle off my knife.

Up another tree and weakened by a loss of blood, the lynx now grew more vicious. I retied the knife to the pole and pushed it into the animal's mouth once again, drawing more blood. The lynx jumped out of the tree and ran away. My dogs gave chase. I ran to follow, but the lynx came back at me from behind a live oak thicket, old Beaver in hot pursuit. Just as it leaped at me with its glaring, green eyes, I hit it on the back of the head with a mesquite branch. Old Beaver gripped the neck of the lynx in a life and death struggle. The pup stood off at a safe distance, a kind of canine "cheerleader," and barked as loud as it could.

I ran back to the tree and retrieved my knife, waited for my chance, and plunged it into the lynx's neck, just behind one ear. Old Beaver was badly injured, but he looked at me with an expression of canine victory.

I skinned the lynx and took his head and hide home as trophies. Seeing the animal was very full, I cut him open to see what he had been eating for lunch. I found three whole turkey feet in his stomach.

Home again, my father bound up old Beaver's wounds, and turning to me said, "Don't you ever risk a thing like that again."

That was the first time, and the last time that I ever tried to kill a Mexican lynx.

Marriage and Family

When I was nineteen years of age, I married Rachel Eliza Banta. We had seven children in all: **Minnie Evelyn** ('92)*, Dora Claire ('95), Angeline Epsy ('97), Claude Merritt ('02), Alma Mae ('04), Leah Violet ('06), and Daymon Slator ('12). Much of my life I have recorded in my diary, so I will open a few of its pages for you to peruse at your leisure.

Springtime in Texas

This spring so far is such a wet spring, and how quickly everything is growing. We have an excellent garden, and corn, etc are growing nicely. The grass is green, in the vales and hills, and the sweet perfume of wild flowers, makes the air fragrant. All the beauty of springtime fills our breast with visions of happiness. So beautifully it prefigures, resurrection from the tomb, and the final consummation of God's purpose in the earth.

The sighs of the vernal wind, as it rustles through the leaves, seems to tell me in a voice, soft but distinctly, that man was created for a higher purpose in life, and that he should not waste his energies on trifles. It tells me that time like a river is flowing into the Great ocean of Eternity. – that it is forever passing, and that a moment passed never returns It tells me that time is not to be wasted, but that the moments should be improved. It also tells me that procrastination is the great besetting evil of humanity. What else does the wind's moaning sigh bring about besides these messages?

... Diary, Spring, 1897

Bob the Dog

For years I had an old mongrel dog named Bob. This old dog had a fierce hatred for snakes… any old kind of snake. He had been bitten so many times by poisonous snakes that every new time that he would get bit by a snake he would swell up in every place that he had previously been bit. He looked all lumpy after each bite. After being bit he would go out under the barn and just stay there until all the swelling went down, then he would come out as good as new, ready to go again.

* Author's Note: Minnie was this author's grandmother. She and "Little Sister" Leah belonged to a "quilting bee," a club that made quilts. Several pages below are the names of members who collaborated to make one quilt (see #30).

One time we were down on the creek about a mile south of our place looking for tree squirrels, which were a delicacy that we liked served with dumplings. Old Bob was running around sniffing at practically everything, when suddenly he got rather excited. He was sniffing under a pile of limbs and leaves when ZAP! a head darted out and got him on the cheek. He grabbed that snake out and bit and shook it until all the life had ebbed from the reptile. He had been bit by a copperhead, which is a dull copper color, and of course has no way of warning before it strikes as does the rattlesnake.

Old Bob then headed under the barn, after we got back home, and stayed there until the swelling went away.

Another time in the corn fields, we were throwing the bundles up on the wagon, then one person would sort them in order that we would have a neat load. As I finished one shock and went to the next one, I tossed the bundles up on the wagon, I then noticed that one of the bundles had the tie-string broken. I started to reach under the shock to get the tie-string, when a white object bolted by me. I then heard the deadly ZZZZZZZZZZ! Whenever you hear that sound you freeze, and a cold chill goes up and down your back. Believe me you will never know the fright of that sound until you have experienced it. Old Bob took the bite right between the eyes. LUCKY ME!

We took old Bob up to the house and sterilized his wound with kerosene, and off he trotted to spend his usual stint under the barn. That time old Bob finally took on a monster that must have been too big for him, for he took a bite that his old body could not handle, and he died. I could hear the rattling of the monster down in the pit: the rattles were course, deep and rough; those rattles were very OLD.

Christmas in Texas

What a beautiful season of the year, 'tis Christmas and all of the family are congregating at John and Angeline Banta's household for the holidays.

We stopped at Kerrville and selected a few presents for our friends and relatives. We believe that much good is often accomplished in bestowing upon our loved ones little assurances of our love and affection especially on Christmas or New Years. Yet we are aware that 'every good gift and every perfect gift is from above and cometh down from the Father of lights with whom is no variableness neither shadow of turning.' Now we leave Kerrville, cross the beautiful Guadalupe, its banks covered with beautiful cypresses, and are going at a rattling pace, to our journey's end.

The sun is setting. Beautiful it is indeed. Lengthened shadows fall in the valley while the summits of the hills are covered with golden light. But 'it is the sunset of life gives me mystical lore'. Now the sun is less than 18° below the horizon and twilight prevails. Well twilight is of two kinds, the light perceived before the rising sun, or after the setting of the sun. So the dim 'twilight of Probability' in life, in some instances may increase in brightness and in others darken into midnight gloom.

At about 8 P.M. we arrived at father-in-law's home. [Next day] it is the day before Christmas. We must have a 'Christmas tree'. We are fond of amusing the children... Lula [Magill] and I go to Centre Point, make the necessary purchases and return. Others prepared a tree. It is soon dressed, ah! 'Life is a bountiful tree, heavy laden with beautiful fruit.' It reminds us of the fact, also that Christ is the Great Tree of Life, —immortal life.— The gifts,—well heaven had no brighter gift than the Son of God himself. Then, there is the Bible, and the virtues, Faith, Hope, Love etc. Manifold indeed are the great blessings bestowed upon us. The lights remind us that Christ is the light of the world, and we are commanded to so walk as to reflect that light. Well, we might see many beautiful figures: but let us pass on. Old Grandma McDonald, Bro. Banta's mother-in-law*, bowed down with her over 'four score years and ten', was helped into the room to view the tree. The sight would have made a beautiful picture. It pictured frail humanity bowing at the tree of Life to receive the blessed gifts to be bestowed upon the children of the faithful after the resurrection.

* Author's Note: Rebecca Angeline's mother, Rachel Axley McDonald, died in 1878. This was John's *mother*, not his mother-in-law. Born Eliza Barker in 1806, she married Zachariah McDonald after the death of her husband Isaac Banta. Evidently Leonard didn't know the whole story of his in-laws (see Appendix 4).

On the day after Christmas, there were still a goodly crowd of us here. Grandma said she never expected to see us again... she is very feeble. We spend the evening in a very profitable manner:

Seth Banta – Webster's Oration on the Death of Mr. White;

Leonard Passmore – Shakespeare's Death of Caesar;

Angie Magill – Why Should the Spirit of Mortal be Proud;

Lula Magill – The New Teacher;

Hardin Oatman – The Crowded Street;

Hugh Magill – "Revenge";

"Young" John O. Banta – Peace and Contentment.

... Diary, Dec. 24-26, 1898

In about 1918, after all our family had grown up and gone off, we sold out all our Gillespie county holdings and moved to Voca, where I purchased 800 acres from one Mr. C.A. Corbell.

A Dream of Things to Come

Like Nebuchadnezzar, the Babylon king of old, I lay upon my bed and pondered over the things to come in the past [sic] hereafter. I was thinking in particular of the great strides of human achievement the last few years and was wondering what the future would bring forth.

In this state of mind, I dropped into slumber calmly and in my dreams there appeared to me a "Being Beauteous" arrayed in the finest apparel. Upon her head was a crown of gold upon which was engraved the letters set in diamonds her name, "Fantasma" which I interpreted to mean "The Queen of Dreams" -- as I viewed, held in wonder, this wondrous visitant she said to me in tones as musical as a sound of dripping waters: "Come with me and I will lift the veil from your eyes, and behold! You shall see the reality now hit by the vista of years."

Then I saw in the distance what appeared to be huge metal grasshoppers bowing as if on prayer carpets, but looking more closely they were numerous derricks, and I heard the thud and lumbering of drilling tools. Taking up our journey to whence the sound emanated, I beheld a magnificent gushing where the oil came glistening above the derrick, spouting fortune in the hands of its promoters.

Then Fantasma, standing with her hand uplifted as if to pronounce a benediction said:

"Katemcy the beautiful, fair to behold,

Resplendent in riches like Croesus of old --

A city of love, of peace and good will,

Your virtue the Heart of fair Texas doth fill!

129

Fredonia, devoid of rebelliousness now,
Hath traded her sword for that coveted plough!
In silicon sand are the prophecies told,
Now sing of bluebonnets, as did men of old!

Then I looked upon the visage of my consort, like the mist of the morning she vanished from my view. Such was my dream.*

... Diary, April 21, 1925

* Author's Note: It is evident from the content and tone of this piece that Leonard Jackson Passmore had read Boethius' *Consolation of Philosophy* (1st c. A.D.). These Texas pioneers were not ignorant plainsmen. Though his poetry leaves something to be desired, he was quite obviously an educated man.

30
Minnie Evelyn Passmore
1892-1973

I don't know how I developed that Spoonerism, but I always told folks that I was born in 1492. I was really born in 1892! My father was a farmer and a teacher... not in that order. My mother was a member of the large Banta family that lived in nearby Mason, Texas.

El Torito

I was twelve years older than my sister Alma (b. 1904), fourteen years older than Leah (b. 1906), whom I always called "Little Sister." We lived on a farm near the San Saba River, south of Brady, Texas. It was a short walk from our house to the barn, where I had to go every day to milk the cows. Little Sister and Alma would usually tag along to "help." Well, one day we were walking along, but our little bull calf was sprawled out across the path and wouldn't budge. There were too-tall weeds on either side, and we just had to get that bullock out of the way. No matter what I did, he wouldn't move. I insulted him; I poked him; I even kicked him. He wouldn't budge. Then I decided to step over him. Just when I got one foot over him, he stood up! That's how I became the "Queen of the Rodeo." I rode that bucking bull for a good minute or so, balancing myself with an empty milk pail in each hand. It was better than any of those mechanical bulls you see in the bars nowadays. Anyway, I'm not going to tell you how it ended. Little Sister and Alma laughed so hard they got side aches. That wasn't the kind of ache that I got.

Alvie

When I first saw that traveling salesman in the white suit, as we sat on the stoop of the Christadelphian church camp near Lyndon's ranch, I told Alma, "That man is mine!"

He wasn't mine yet, but he soon would be. I married Alvie Stewart in 1913. We had three boys: **Leonard** ('14), Dorman ('16'), and Othello ('20).

Premonitions

Some people said I was clairvoyant, and it was probably true. Sometime after the Great Depression, when all of our boys were in their teens, the movie theaters started having what they called "bank nights," in which they would hold a kind of lottery, based on the audience's ticket stubs. One night I told Jack he should go to the movies, but he refused, saying, "I got a dollar, but if I squeeze a nickel, the buffalo will holler." (Jack was one of the stingiest kids who ever lived.)

131

He didn't go, but we later learned they had called his name to the tune of $100. Another time I told Dorman to go, but he didn't want to, so Jack went instead. This time they called Dorm's name, for $300. Then one night, Othello and his friends were planning to go to a dance. I wrote a note that read, "In case of emergency, contact Mrs. A.C. Stewart," and wrote my phone number on it. One of the girls had to get home early, so 'Theller's friend drove her in our car. He must not have had his "mind on the driving, his hands on the wheel, nor his snoopy eyes on the road ahead," for he smacked right into a train that was stopped across the road. No one was hurt, but our car sure took a beating. That boy's father surely gave him a beating, too.

I guess I should have spoken up that morning when Alvie went out with Daymon to open up that water well. I really had a bad feeling, but I couldn't quite pinpoint what it was…

As long as I lived in Voca, I belonged to the Voca Quilting Bee.

Quilting Club 1962-63: Lilly Spiller, Effie Mayo,
Winnie Deans, Willie Brown, Maggie Clevenger,
Hazel Flournoy, Georgia Locklear, Myrtle Behrens,
Lona Miller, Minnie E. Stewart.

THE NAMES ON THE QUILT*

Ruby Liverman	Edith Trammel	Mrs. W. M. Deans		Peggy Edminton
	Minneta Edminton 1947			
Ollie Whitely	Mrs. Yarbrough June 25, 1947	Leona Holloway		Lillie Spiller
	Minnie Brown			
Evelyn Stewart	Lillie Edminton	Mrs. Mayo 1947		Mrs. Elgin McLarsan
	Fay Wood			
Lena Wallace	Leah Henderson	Georgia Locklear 1947		Nancy Willis
	Verna Boswell			

* Author's Note: I have often wondered about the Names on the Quilt. Who were those ladies? What became of them? Was one of them the same old lady who jokingly put ice in my shirt pocket after church, one summer while we were staying at my grandmother's house? I will never know (or will I?), but I reckon Minnie (Evelyn) *et alia* were the last of the true Pioneer Women.

The Milors

The Milor family originated in Milor, a village in Cornwall. As such, it is a habitation name, rather than an occupational name. St. Melor, son of King Melian of Cornwall and Haurilla, daughter of Earl Rivold of Devonshire, gave his name to the village. However, he embraced the Christian faith and was murdered barbarously because of it. The family was originally from Flanders. As there were no distinct spelling rules at the time, it has been spelled variously as Mellers, Mellors, Meller, Mellor, Melliar, and others.

Samuel Meller, b. 2 March 1721, Dublin
m. Cathryn
John Meller
m. Margret
Thomas Meller, b. 5 December 1764
or
William Meller, b. 6 February 1767
m. Jane b. 16 January 1771.
John William Meller / Meeler / Mayler → Milor (b 1795)
m. Amanda Morgan (1807-1879)
William L. Milor, b. 1826 (NC/TN) - d. 1885 (TX)
m. Minerva E. Best (1829-1882)
Charles Washington Milor b. 1862 (Ark) – d. 1946 (CA)
m. Allie Lee Stewart
Albert Roberson Milor, b. 1895 (OK) - d. 1969 (CA)
m. Gatie Mildred Houck
Faye Marilyn Milor, b. 1918 (OK) – d. 1998 CA
m. Leonard J. Stewart

31
John William Milor
1795-1847

My name is Jonathan William Millefleur. I was born in Monkstown, a little village just to the south of Dublin. My family were devout Baptists, and since we were living in a mainly Catholic part of town, that made us an endangered species. Yet like many teenaged boys, I had my doubts.

When I was a schoolboy, I would climb up to the top of Saint Patrick's Tower with my friend "Key Row." His name was Keough Roe, but everyone called him "Cheops," because he was so interested in the Egyptian pyramids. As for me, I preferred to "Greekify" his name to "Chi-Ro" – XP.*

I looked up to Key Row because he was a year older than me. Not only that, but he had the key to the tower. His uncles owned the distillery where the tower was located. It used to be a windmill, but with the industrial revolution they switched to coal, so the tower went out of use… as a windmill, that is.

They still made good whiskey, though. We would take a bottle of Key Row's whiskey and some Dutch tobacco and make a grand ol' Saturday night of it.

My father couldn't have taken a strap to me, even if he had known what I was up to. He was off with Wellington, fighting against Napoleon. He was getting too old to fight, but the British had conscripted him when I was about eight, because he was good at logistics. We hadn't heard from him for a long time… I wondered if he was all right.

"How high up are we?" I asked my host, the first time we went up in the Tower.

"One hundred eleven feet," he answered, in a matter-of-fact tone.

"How do you know that?" I challenged him.

"If you take one of those metal triangles that we use in school, you know, the one whose sides measure 3-4-5, you can calculate the height," he explained.

"How?"

"You go down to the ground and walk out some distance, holding the bottom of the triangle even with the ground, until you can sight along the long side to the top of the tower. Then you measure how far away you are."

* Author's Note: Chi-Ro (spelled 'XP' in Greek) was a symbol of Christ that Constantine
saw before he went into battle. He won the battle, so he converted to Christianity.

"How far is that?"

"One hundred forty-eight feet. Proportionately, that is the '4' side of the triangle. The '3' side is the height of the Tower."

"Hmm, One-hundred forty-eight divided by four equals..."

"Thirty-seven," he interrupted. "Thirty-seven times three equals..."

"One hundred eleven," I answered correctly.

We kept on drinking and smoking. I asked him about Saint Patrick, the namesake of our magnificent drinking perch. Where had all those snakes and frogs gone, I wondered out loud.

"There is only one variety of frog native to Ireland," he said, "and they're still here. There never were any snakes. Saint Patrick drove out the Celtic goddesses whose symbols were snakes."

I asked him what he thought about the war with France. He told me that the French victories were only "Pyrrhic victories," which meant that Napoleon would lose in the end. As it turned out, he was right.

In the days to come, I would have my own Pyrrhic victories. You see, I was having struggles with my faith. I won a few rounds, but in the end, it was the Catholics who would drive me out, just as old Saint Patrick had driven out the snakes and frogs in days gone by.

Wafers

One Sunday morning my sister Margrett and I decided to go to a Catholic church service to see what all the fuss was about. We went to the Church of the Holy Trinity, their main cathedral. They had these cute little wafers that they used to conduct the Holy Eucharist. The people lined up, the priest broke the "bread," and he gave it to each one of them who was older than about eight years old.

"That's odd," I told Margrett. "They baptize babies, but they won't let them take communion until they are old enough to take responsibility for their own sins."

"Not only that," she rejoined. "The priest drinks all their wine by himself."

"Must be some life, being a priest," I snickered. "Look at that! He has the letters 'HIS' embroidered on the back of his gown."

"Probably if they let women be priests, they would write 'HERS' on their backs," she said.

I wondered if they would ever let women be priests. They seemed fairly dogmatic in that category.

I also wondered why they would pray to Saint Mary and all those other saints. My mother never prayed to anyone but God himself. One thing that I liked was that after you died, if you didn't get into Heaven, you could go to Purgatory for a while until you earned enough points to get where you wanted to go.

One night I was in a pub. It was 1814, I think. Key Row was there, drinking Smithwick's ale. We got to talking about the Irish language.

"I was thinking about the other night in the Tower," he began. "We were drinking 'Old '72' whiskey. It's like the Tower of Babel."

"How's that?" I queried.

"You know, Fennius Farsaid was one of 'The Old 72.'"

"Who? Which 72?"

"Fennius Farsaid. He was one of the seventy-two princes who built the Tower of Babel."

"Oh, *that* old seventy-two. Of course!"

"He went to Scythia after the Tower collapsed, and from there he sent out a retinue of 72 scholars to study the confused languages."

"Seems like he was fixed on the numbers seven and two."

"When the studies were complete, he distilled all the world's languages, just like our distillery. Then he wrote 'The Secret Language of the Poets.'"

"Di-still and know that I am God."

"Then he invented the Ogham alphabet.

"What's that?"

"Each letter is named after a tree: alder, birch, elder, fern, gooseberry, hazel, pine, rowan, whitethorn, yew, and so on."

"That's only ten letters," I remarked.

"And so on, I said."

"Oh, right."

"His son married the daughter of Pharaoh Cingris. Her name was Scota, and that's how Scotland got its name."

"Do tell. How about Ireland?"

"Their son was named Goidel. A snake bit him, so they took him to Moses, who prayed hard and touched his rod on the lad's wound. The snake bite left a green ring on the boy, so they called him Goidil Glas ('Glas' means 'green' in Irish).

"I think I'll have another *glass* of Smithwick's. But you didn't tell me how Ireland got its name." *

* Author's Note: The name "Ireland" came from Ir, one of the sons of Milesius, a king of Spain who colonized Hibernia. His mother, a daughter of another Pharaoh, was also named Scota.

Just at that moment, the Blackbird of Belfast flew in and sat down beside me. She began to recite death tales, battle tales, adventures, stories of cattle raids, stories of voyages, visions, wooings, and destructions. It was time to stop drinking and go home. (Anyway, the Blackbird had flown off somewhere.)

On the way back home, Key Row told me he wanted to make a stop in the Night Quarter. He had several friends whose sisters worked there, and he wanted to convince one or all of them to come home to their families. Their names were Millie, Kitty, and Flo.

We called at the home of Mrs. Mack, who told us that Millie was busy "with a friend." Mrs. Collins said something nearly the same of Kitty. Mrs. Arnett said we could come in and wait, but when Key Row saw that Flo's "friend" was Lord Mayor Beresford (enjoying some "princely hospitality") he became irate, swinging his walking stick around wildly, and finally he broke the lady's chandelier.

The Sub-Constable came and carted us off to the gaol. There we were grilled by the Chief Dublin Magistrate, who questioned our identities. Key Row and Millefleur came off broadly as Keel Row and Miller, Kehoe and Meller, or Kimbrough and Mellior. I stuck with the last one, but I had to wait for my mother to come to the court the next day to pay my one-shilling fine for disturbing the peace.

The Venison of the Sun

In 1815 I went to Ospidéal Rotunda, the Hospital for the Relief of Poor Lying-in Women. Because of poor ventilation, one out of six children died within nine days after birth. This was the reason why a Church of Ireland priest continually roamed the corridors of the Rotunda. They baptized infants, you know.

My uncle John's wife Frances was one of those lying-in women. Her baby, like so many others, was not destined to see the light of the sun. Uncle John, being a Baptist, wouldn't let the priest baptize his baby. The priest berated him, demanding that he should explain why a "Baptist" would not allow his baby to be baptized.

After the funeral, and before Frances was released from the hospital, I went across the river with Uncle John to the Brazen Head pub. There the Guinness flowed out of St. James' Gate.

I asked him why he wouldn't let the priest baptize his child. You never know what help a baby might need in getting into Heaven.

"It is not meet to butcher the Sacred Cow of the Catholics," he said, "but we are Baptists. For the last hundred years we have adhered to the five *Solas* of the Reformation: *Sola Fide, Sola Scriptura, Sola Christus, Sola Gratia*, and *Sola Deo Gloria*."

"By faith alone," I translated, knowing a bit of our Baptist creed myself; "by scripture, through Christ, by grace, and with glory to God."

"The Unison of the *Solas*," he concluded.

"Unison Solis," I mused, my Guinness beginning to take effect; "the Venison of the Sun."

The Suitors

After the battle of Waterloo, Duke Wellington didn't need my father anymore, so he sent him home to Monkstown. There, outside our house, lurked a company of strange and evil men, all of whom hoped that my father would be killed in the war so they could marry my mother Jane. They didn't recognize him as William but thought he was another suitor, like them.

Father William devised a test to drive them all from in front of our home, and at the same time to deprive them of their hopes.

"Who made the Wellington Boot?" he asked them.*

"Hoby of St. James Street, 1815," they replied, being well-informed, though none would have been classy enough to own such a boot, much less wear it.

"What contains the sum total of all religion and morals?"

"The Lord's Prayer," they answered, having kept the pace with news of the Duke and his witty remarks.

"How did one cavalry unit get out of a sandstorm in western Spain?"

"They used jars of raspberry jam as markers so the riders wouldn't lose their way," the evil suitors responded, more out of logic than knowledge, for they had not been there in Spain.

"What is Millefleur's Maxim?" he asked, turning the debate to his own purview.

"Being born in Monkstown does not make one a monk," they said. Not one of them qualified in any way for the vows.

"What did Wellington promise Millefleur's son, when he found the lad crying because he didn't want to go to school?"

"To take care of his toad," said one, who somewhat resembled a toad in his own right.

"And here, gentlemen, is the toad which Duke Wellington has given me to return to young John, my son."

Possession of that lovely toad was better than stringing the strongest bow, better than firing the straightest arrow through a dozen axe handles. With that the suitors one by one and all together left Monkstown, never to set eyes on my mother Jane again.

After my father came home, I embraced the Baptist faith with a passion. I embraced it so much that I am afraid I fulfilled the prophecy of Saint Patrick, made way back when we were up in that tower.

* Author's Note: This boot, a simplified version of the Hessian boot, evolved into the cowboy boot in the USA.

I began to preach on the street corners… not a wise thing to do when all your neighbors are Catholics. Eventually they caught up with me and forced me to leave Monkstown. In fact, my reputation as a Baptist preacher had spread so far and wide that I realized I might not be safe anywhere in Ireland.

So it was that in 1816 I bade farewell to my father, my mother and sister, and boarded a ship for the New World.

There I met Amanda Morgan, married her, and settled down to a new life. Talk about being born again!

32
William L. Milor
1826-1885

Our family came to Huntsville, Tennessee when I was about ten years old. When I was old enough, and of steady mind, I became a Baptist preacher, traveling all over the country on horseback.

The Arkansas Traveler

On one of my missionary trips I find myself in Arkansas. I come upon a man in his cabin, whose hair is white as the winter snow, though it were only April. This fellow says he is a hundred and twenty-five years old. He sits there playing on his fiddle "The Bonnie Earl O'Moray." *

"Thou shalt rise up before the hoary head," I recall the Good Book says. I figure that means you spend the night at his house and wake up early before he does. And so I asks him, "Sir, can you find me a bed?"

"Why don't you sleep on the road?" he sasses me. Maybe he's not as hoary as all that, methinks.

"Then could you point me the way to a tavern or an inn?"

Just then the rain comes down like a waterfall, which seems not to bother him, though he sees my depressed countenance, at which he says, "All right, you may come inside."

His roof leaks like a sieve.

"Why don't you fix your roof?" I asks.

"It is too wet and cold," he explains.

"Then why don't you fix it on some sunny morning, when the air is nice and dry?"

"Why should I?" he retorts. "When the days are bright and fair, my cabin never leaks a drop!"

At last he pours me some coffee before I go to bed. I wake the next morning soaked through and through, but "before the hoary head." Before I leave, I thanks that gentleman for his kind hospitality.

* See Appendix 2.

143

In 1848 I married **Minerva Best**. We had seven children: John Carroll ('49), William Henry ('54), James Franklin ('56), **Charles William** ('62), Thomas Marion ('65), Amanda Anna ('67), and Minerva Jane ('70). That last one was born in Arkansas, where we moved, thanks to that old geezer playing his fiddle in a leaky cabin.

William, John, Charles
James, Thomas

And so, like the wind we moved. I became a minister at the Hibbit Church, about four miles Northeast of Gainesville, Texas. Then in 1874 we traveled to Indian Territory, for I was to be a missionary to the Indians. I took my family Bible with me.

33

Charles William Milor

1862-1946

I cried like a baby when the War Between the States broke out. That's because I *was* a baby. I was born in Camden, Arkansas, in March of 1862. It was halfway between Nashville and Dallas. After the war (1874), we moved to Indian Territory. I was twelve years old at the time. My mother died when I was eighteen years old. My father died when I was 21.

Trapping and Hunting

After my parents died, I did a lot of freighting and trapping with my brother Marion, up in the northeast part of Oklahoma (when it was Indian territory), and also out in west Texas.

One November day in 1887, we (Charles, Marion, and our sister Amanda's husband Pressley Tennyson) set out to get supplies for a camping trip. We took two mules, a wagon, food, three Winchester rifles, and three .45 cal. six-shooters, three thousand rounds of ammunition, four hundred bottles of strychnine, and thirty beaver traps. We left Purcell and went northwest, stopping at Cobb Creek. We soon knew the meaning of the old saying that warns us about beauty being dangerous.

After we had been in camp for three days a band of Indians found us. Their chief was named Old Washee. With him were fifteen of his sons. The other men were out trapping, so I had to defend our wagon and supplies on my own. I was determined to use all the muscle that my twenty-two years possessed to protect our supplies and later take to the bushes for gun play, if necessary, to protect my breath supply.

Two of the young Indians who had formed a circle about the wagon could talk. They asked me to give them everything they could think of. When I refused they bunched up to growl and grunt. Meanwhile, my two companions returned to camp with their guns at the ready. I implored them not to kill the Indians if we could find another way out. This seemed to soften the Indians somewhat. They insisted, however, that we leave that camp, and followed us until dark to make sure we did.

Up on Calvary Creek there were thousands of turkeys, plenty of beaver, and a few antelopes. The river was dammed up every few hundred yards by the beavers, so we could cross it at any place in the valley. We trapped all up and down the river, catching quite a few beavers, and poisoning from three to fifteen wolves every night.

Next we camped on the Washita River near where Cheyenne is now located, on the old battle grounds where General Custer and his men killed the old Cheyenne Chief Black Kettle and most of his tribe. About ten acres of ground were covered with Indian bones and the rifle pits [fox holes] were still waist deep. Oklahoma should make that place a state park.*

The first night in this camp I invented Indian-head coffee. Going after a bucket of water, I picked up an old Indian skull, washed it off nice and clean and dropped it into the bucket of water. It was night and I was not a heavy drinker; I did not drink any water. Of course my companions both liked their coffee with supper, but I didn't want any that night. I got mine the next morning, but it wasn't coffee! While I slept, my brothers had filled the bucket with mud! Phew!**

Judge Roy Bean

I once lived for two years in Pecos, Texas, where I met and became a good friend to Judge Roy Bean, though he was quite a bit older than I. He was a colorful character who had once escaped from jail in San Diego, when his friends smuggled him a knife in his meal of tamales. He used it to dig out of his cell and escaped to San Gabriel.

After the war, he bought a saloon near Eagle's Nest, Texas. He named it "The Jersey Lilly," after Emilie Charlotte Langtry, a famous actress. One of the Texas Rangers noticed that there was no justice for several hundred miles, so Roy Bean became a justice of the peace. All his cases were settled by fines. There was no jail in town, so those who couldn't pay their fines were simply chained to an oak tree out back.

One train passenger rudely tossed Judge Bean a $20 gold piece in payment for a glass of beer. He refused to give the man change. When the man protested, Judge Bean fined him $19.95 for "contempt of court." The other five cents would pay for the beer. Any further protest would result in a doubling of the fine. Needless to say, the man was on the next train out of there.

* Author's Note: Washita Battlefield, about halfway between Oklahoma City and Amarillo, Texas, is now designated a national historical site.

** Author's Note: I think this is a tall tale. Accounts differ widely as to how many Indians were killed in the 1868 battle. About 6,000 Indians were there for their winter camp, which Custer attacked. Some Indians said only thirteen of them were killed, while Gen. Custer reported killing between 106 and 140. How many skulls were left there is anybody's guess.

Family Life

In 1891, I joined the land run to Oklahoma and homesteaded in Cowden, which is in Washita County. In that same year I married Alice Lee Stewart, whose parents were early settlers there too. They ran a general store in Cowden. We had six children: **Albert** ('95), Nellie ('03), Benjamin (Gene) ('05), Marvin ('07), Marzie ('09), and Carroll ('13).

We kept the farm in Cowden and lived there except for the two years we went back to Indian Territory. That's where Albert was born. He was so little (he weighed only three pounds) that we fixed up a bed for him in a shoe box. After that we moved back to Cowden and built a half dugout (a house that is half-way buried under ground, in case of tornadoes). Finally, we built a two-room house above ground. We stayed on this farm in Cowden until we moved to California in 1930, thirty-five years later.

Country Life

In 1893, my brother John organized the Valley View Baptist Church in Cowden. He had been a pioneer missionary to the Oklahoma Indians, though he was living in Gainesville, Texas. All the members of the Milor family belonged to that church. We always baptized people in the Washita River.

We really enjoyed visiting friends and relatives. When we saw a family coming to visit, we would walk down to the road to meet them. The grown-ups would ride back to the house in the wagon, and all the children would get out and walk back. I remember seeing my first car one day. We were in the watermelon patch and one of the neighbors rode up in his car. It had a crank on the side of the engine.

In 1923 our house burned down, and we lived in the barn and the cellar until a new house was built. We were all working in the field when the house burned. Allie had just been to the house a while before. No one ever knew the cause of the fire, but we figured it was a mouse that had got into the matches.*

The new house had a gas stove to cook on and gas lamps instead of kerosene lamps, and we had a gas-operated Maytag washer. We were probably the first people in the county to have such modern conveniences.

* Author's Note: This story brings home the realistic, not merely contrived, aspect of Billy Collins' poem, "The Country."

Outlaws

There were outlaws, as well as Indians, living down by the Washita River, which wasn't far from our house. One night we had gone to church, and when we came home we noticed that a dresser was out from the wall a little. It was across the corner of the room, but we thought it was out a little more than it should have been, but we left it and went to bed.

The next morning, we found we had been robbed of much of our clothes and all the money we had. There had been someone hiding behind the dresser when we came home. I knew who did it, but I wasn't about to accuse anyone. That same night there had been a lot of robberies thereabouts. No one would say anything for fear of them coming back and doing them harm. People were afraid of the outlaws.

One bunch of outlaws were the Hughes gang. They had a ranch on the other side of the river. Those brothers were always robbing the bank at Cobb, Oklahoma, which was quite close. As soon as any money was put in the bank, they would rob it. Once the brothers were chased down to the river after a robbery. They had a car which they ran right into the river. They left the car and escaped. My uncle said that every time someone would go down near where the Hughes lived, they could always see someone peeking around a tree or looking out of a window. Once he saw a man hanging from a tree – and scooted out of there as fast as he could. No one ever investigated, but everyone knew it was done by the Hughes Brothers.

Bad Language

One night a man rode into my yard on his horse while I was asleep. Allie went to the door, and the man wanted to know where my nephew lived. Allie tried to wake me so I could tell him, but I was sound asleep… Zzzz. The man got irritated and started swearing and rode off. I was half-way awake by then, and I heard what he said. The next morning, I got the surrey out and had my two sons get the horses hitched to it. I took my gun and had the boys go with me to their cousin's house. I arrested the man for swearing in front of my wife and family. I couldn't stand for anyone to use that kind of language. The man's trial came up six months later; I went to court to testify against him. The judge let him off with a slap on the wrist, because the man said I was sleeping so soundly that I couldn't possibly have heard him swear those words.

In 1930 we moved to California to live with our son Henry, who was living alone with his little boy. He couldn't work and take care of Sonny at the same time, so he needed our help.

34
Albert Roberson Milor
1895-1969

I was born in Indian Territory, eighteen hundred and ninety-five. Twelve years later, when Oklahoma became a state, they changed the name of the place to Duncan.

In those days Oklahoma territory was expanding. They had land runs, in which the "sooners" (people that got there *sooner*) could stake out their claims and start a homestead. My father was a Baptist minister to the Indians.

Starting a Family

Gatie Houck and I lived within two miles of one another all our lives. We went to school and church together since we were very little children. We were all good friends with the children and went to school and church together.

When we got bigger, Gatie played the organ in the Valley View Church (she had learned to play as a little girl, for somehow her family had an organ in the house). Gatie and I were married in 1916 at her parents' home in Cowden (probably because they had that organ). The wedding was quite a celebration for the two families. I had come courting her in a buggy, of course.

Gatie and Albert Milor

When I was a young man, my father went down to Wichita, Texas, to work in the oil fields. The whole family went with him, but we soon moved back to Oklahoma, settling first in Cowden (which is near Cloud Chief), then in Mountain View.

I worked at the cotton gin for a good many years. We bought groceries at a little store nearby; I had a charge account there. I paid some on it each Saturday when I got paid. Then I always bought a bag of candy and brought it home for the kids.

We lived in Mountain View, but on Sundays we would drive over to Cowden, about forty-five minutes away. My mom would always go out to the yard and catch a couple of chickens (they roamed around in the yard), and she would wring their necks (hold them by the head and swing them round and round until the head came off). Then they floundered around on the ground, headless, a while before they died. She then put them in scalding water so the feathers would come off easy, then she plucked the feathers off and prepared them for cooking.

There was a big pot-bellied stove in the kitchen, where there was also a long table. The kids always crowded in behind the table, and if they wanted to leave the table before everyone was finished, they had to crawl under the table and between everyone's legs to get out.

The farm wives always had a quilt hung up to work on, so if there was ever a visiting, time was spent quilting while they visited (except on Sundays, when work wasn't done on the quilt).

Old Night

Cowden is near the Washita River where many Indians lived. They would often come to our door begging for food. The farm people always gave them something to eat so they would go away. One Indian named Old Night was a regular visitor to our home. He always showed up at supper time and was given food. Then he went to the corner of the room and sat and ate. When he finished, he just got up and left.

Moving to California

Sometime in 1930 my dad decided to move to California. My brother Henry was living there, working for the B.F. Goodrich Tire Company. Henry was divorced, but he still had a little son to take care of. My dad was 68 years old, too old to take care of his farm alone. So he and Mom and my brother Woody decided to go out to California to live with Henry.

* Author's Note: This is an odd reminder (?) of the TV series OA, in which the heroine, in a David Lynch-like theater scene is connected to a giant octopus named Old Night, which uses her voice to speak to the audience.

Life and times in Oklahoma were getting mighty rough, so Gatie and I decided to move to California, too. Gatie didn't like leaving her family behind; you couldn't just hop in a car and drive, drive, drive, like you can now. She never saw her mother again.

We arrived in Montebello and lived with Mom and Dad, which was a bit cramped. I had a policeman friend from Oklahoma who was now working as a guard at Chrysler Motors in Maywood. He let me know that they may be hiring, so I applied for a job. I was accepted and worked there until I retired. I was an inspector of cars as they came off the assembly line as a finished product.

We bought a house on Sixth Street in Montebello. It had two rental units and a garage, with a big pepper tree in the front yard. Mrs. Fontaine was our long-term tenant. There were several short-term tenants in the other unit. Our life was constantly punctuated by sirens, for there was a fire station down the street.

Chief Rainwater

Gatie's brother Calvin married a girl named Flo Rainwater. I think that name was an Americanized form of the German family name Reinwasser, meaning "pure water." Anyway, Flo's brother was named Olen, whose wife was Cherokee Eleanor, a half Indian. He rode an Indian Chief motorcycle, so we used to call him "Chief Rainwater." He came to visit us in Montebello. He had fixed up his motorcycle as one of those "touring" bikes with saddlebags, windshield, and the whole kit 'n' kaboodle.

Catching a Bird

Do you know the best way to catch a bird? You sneak up behind it and put salt on its tail!

The Houcks

My maternal grandmother's maiden name was Houck. Not much is known about this branch of the family, as they can only be traced back as far as *her* (Gatie's) grandfather, William, who was born in Ohio and died in Texas.

> William E. Houck 1840 (OH)-1863 (TX)
> m. Lucinda Alice Fain (or Franklin)
> William Houck 1857 (PA)-1923
> m. Willie Sue Beckner 1880-1933
> Gatie Mildred Houck 1897-1965
> m. **Albert Roberson Milor**

There are several possible origins of the name Houck – Germany, Friesland, and Anglo-Saxon England. Those in the latter case resided at Hooke, at Kingston-upon-Thames. Others with similar names included Richard Hoc (1218), John Hook (1230, in the Pipe Rolls of Berkshire), Reginald de le Hoke, of Wiltshire (in the Hundredorum Rolls, 1273), Robert de Hok, of Somerset, William de Huk, (1296, of Galloway, Scotland), and Margareta del Hoke (in the Yorkshire Tax Rolls, 1379).

The first settlers in America included Jury Houck (New York, 1715-1716), Anthony Houck (Somerset County, Pennsylvania, 1838), and Henry Houck (Maryland, 1844). The most likely candidates for ancestry of William E. Houck (b. 1840) from among these would be Jury Houck. However, records indicate that in 1638 Abraham Temple (see #20, above) brought suit against Mssrs. Humphrey, Howe and Hauk for damage done by their horses.

153

William and Willie Houck

35

Marilyn Faye Milor

1918-1998

Howdy! I was born in Cowden, Oklahoma, where my parents lived. There was no post office there, so the records show that I was born in Cloud Chief.

When I was still little, we moved to Electra, near Wichita, Texas. My grandparents had gone there to work in the oil fields, so we went too. While there, my mom would go out and milk a cow so I would have milk to drink, but she didn't know whose cow it was. She only knew that she needed milk for me. We moved back to Oklahoma after that; my two younger brothers were born there.

Country Life

When we moved to Mountain View, Dad worked at a cotton gin. That is where the cotton from the fields is "ginned," that is, seeds are removed, and the cotton is made into large bales. I remember going to the gin to play on the bales of cotton. They were always lined up on the yard in rows, and we could walk on top of them and jump from one group of bales to another.

On Saturday us kids usually got a dime for our spending money. My brothers would spend their dime and go to the movies, as there was a theater in town. They always showed Western movies, but I didn't care for them, so I didn't go. On Saturday night most of the people went to town, mostly to visit with one another. We sometimes took the car in the afternoon and got a good place to park it and walked back to town at night and the car would be there to sit in when we were not walking up and down the street, visiting with people. Some people did what weekly shopping they had to do that night, for clothing, etc. I had my dime to spend because I didn't go to the show. The dime was spent mostly at the five and ten cent store for candy. Lots of times I went home with a friend and spent the night and we could go to Sunday School together the next day. We always begged our parents to see who could go where.

After church on Sundays, I usually went home with a friend and had dinner and stayed with her until Sunday night church and we went back together. My best friend belonged to the Holiness Church (they may be called the Church of God in some places). They were the people who always spoke in tongues and got so excited and carried away in their services. They actually went down front at the end of services and some rolled on the ground, or on the floor.

The Holiness Church held their revival meetings in the summer, in the park, under a big tent. That was not very far from where we lived, and it was always interesting for us to go to the meetings and watch them. We enjoyed the gospel singing, and also the demonstrations. I usually went with my friend who belonged to that church.

We had a car ever since I can remember, but we walked most of the time. We walked to church, even in winter when it was very cold. We didn't have a lot of snow there, but we had sleet and there were many days when I braved that cold sleet and wind to walk home from school, almost frozen.

Christmas in Oklahoma

We didn't have very much for Christmas. There were electric lights in town, but people didn't put up Christmas trees and decorate them like we do now. We hung stockings and got a little candy and an orange or apple. The best part of Christmas was the Christmas play at church and school.

One Christmas, after us kids were supposedly asleep, there was a loud noise which startled us. We thought it was Santa Claus, and I guess it was. The next morning, we all had little rocking chairs.

Moving to California

I was not too happy about going to a new school where I had no friends. When we got to California, I was starting in the second semester of the eighth grade. In September, I started at Montebello High School. I always got good grades but never enjoyed school. I was just looking forward to getting out of school and getting a job.

Kids didn't date in those days in high school. The only time I went with any boy was to the high school prom when I was a senior. Some of us kids from the Sunday School did have dances in one of our homes almost every Saturday night. That way we learned to dance and enjoyed that very much. That was about our only social activity except church and young peoples' meetings at church.

During my last year of high school my cousin Opal came to live with us. Her dad went to work in the desert (he was a cook for a surveying group), but that was not a good place for a young girl to live, so she lived with us.

When I was in high school, we wore uniform clothes. The girls wore middy blouses and navy skirts the first year; after that, we wore navy skirts and plain white blouses. That way I didn't need a lot of clothes. The only formal I had was for the Senior Prom. That must have been my only graduation present from the folks. I was satisfied because I knew how hard it was for them to buy even that. I was only able to buy the yearbook the last year of school. I got two other gifts for graduation. One was a dollar from a neighbor and the other was a pair of panties [!] from a friend of the family.

Life and Death After High School

After high school (1937) we looked for work but had no luck. We went to dances in the Huntington Park Ballroom, also at the Shrine Auditorium in Los Angeles. If one of my brothers would give us a ride, we would go to the Civic Auditorium in Pasadena. Sometimes we went to a show, or to the beach if it was summer. Then I met Wannie, a girl who lived a few houses east of us.

In the meantime, I had been going with a young man named Denny Flannagan, and we had become engaged. No date had been set for the wedding. We were more or less waiting to decide because he and his family were Catholic, and we were Baptist. We hated to make a problem in either of our families.

We usually went out somewhere on Friday nights, but this particular Friday he for some reason went into West Los Angeles to visit an older sister. On his way home a trash truck collided with his car and he was killed instantly. The driver of the truck had been drinking. I was completely grief stricken. All my future plans had been destroyed in one night.

How I Met Jack Stewart

I finally started going out to dances and going with other boys, but there was no one that interested me. Wannie and I at one time went out with brothers, more or less just to go somewhere. In the summer of 1940, I borrowed a boy's car (I don't know why he let me use it… I didn't know him very well), and I decided to drive over to Brea to visit Wannie, who was staying with her aunt and uncle. When I got there, she wasn't there. I went in and soon Wannie's cousin Jack walked in. He had just come down from San Jose where he was going to college. We went for a little ride (in that other boy's car), just to pass the time. I wasn't too interested in him, although Wannie had told me how special he was. Later, after he went to Texas to visit his grandparents, he came back and called me, saying that he wanted to go out. I was still grieving for my lost love and I tried to put him off. He kept on until I said I would see him.

I found that I had changed my attitude towards him then, and we saw each other almost every night until he went back to college. By that time I was sure I was in love again. He had one more year in college, and we didn't see each other again until Thanksgiving, then again at Christmas time. At that time we decided to get married.*

On January first, 1941, he came over in his dad's car and we drove to Las Vegas without letting anyone know. We got married just a little before midnight and headed right back, because I had to go to work the next day. We only got home at daybreak, and I went off to work that same day.

Faye, Gatie and Albert

* Author's Note: This episode is parodied in *Collected Short Stories*, by E.J. Stewart.

36

Jan E.J. Stewart

1948-

There is a Puritan strand which runs throughout American society. Not everyone adheres to it, but I do… to some extent. I saw it first-hand in my parents: they were saints, but they didn't seem particularly religious; they were just good people. I reckoned that I (at least the older-than-twenty-one me) was a fairly good person. But I didn't hope that I could get to Heaven on my own goodness. Luckily, I would have help. When it came to "thoughts and prayers," I found that "prayers" were usually more effective.

Misa

People often ask me what it is like to live in Japan. I tell them that it's like the little girl with the great big curl, right in the middle of her forehead: when people are good, they are very, very good; when they are bad, they are horrid.

This is the story of one of those people; one who is very, very good. I ended the first part of my story (Section 10, above) with a reference to passing by the brass ring on the Carousel of Life.

I refer to that first phase of my life as the A.M. portion, meaning "Ante Misam." Those were the days before I met Misa. This second P.M., or "Post Misam" portion is the part of my life beginning with the time that I met Misa. She is the "Gold Ring" whom I told you about.

It was a match made in heaven, for those of you who appreciate Symmetry. Each of our families, that is, our respective fathers and mothers, had three children: two girls and a boy. These brothers and sisters subsequently had two children each: a boy and a girl. That is two sets of two girls and a boy, plus six pairs of boys and girls. Beyond that, the symmetry rather fizzles out, but that much, I believe is a good lesson in Symmetry!

Japan (Phase 1)

After our daughter Hillary was born, I finally extricated myself from Chapman College and moved overseas to Japan. Within days I had a bit of a teaching engagement at the YMCA in Daimyo, Fukuoka. There I met Mrs. Itakura, who introduced me, at length, to Fukuoka Jo Gakuin College. It took a few months, but then I started full-time at Daiichi Economics College in Dazaifu. I had several other part-time jobs, at places like Seinan University, Saga Women's Junior College, and "Down-the-Hill."

A Prophecy

One night Misa woke me and said, "Jan, I just had a dream that you were working for a big refrigerator company in Saudi Arabia."

"You're nuts," I told her. "Go back to sleep."

As it turns out, this was one of her prophetic dreams.

America Redux

Things didn't work out in Japan, so we returned to America. Our flight was from Osaka to Vancouver. We crossed the border in Blaine, Washington, where the immigration officer in charge granted Misa a "humanitarian parole" visa. That meant in six months she would have to return to the consulate in Vancouver to apply for permanent residence.

We hung out in Denver for that time. Finally we went back to Vancouver, and Misa got her permanent residence visa. Jobs in Denver were scarce, so we moved to San Francisco. Misa worked in a jewelry store for a while, and for a couple of travel companies.

Teaching jobs were hard to come by in the Bay Area, though I did a brief stint at U.C. Berkeley. One day Misa showed me a newspaper advertisement for teaching in Saudi Arabia. I needed to be doing something constructive, so I went to the interview(s) in Andover, Massachusetts. From there I flew off (they had to de-ice the wings in Boston) to the desert kingdom, teaching at the Military College in Jeddah.

Saudi Arabia (Phase 1)

Misa and Hillary joined me after a few months. We lived in "Rayville," a company compound owned by Raytheon, which also made Gibson air conditioners (and refrigerators... remember that dream?). I will never forget that fateful day when we were in the video rental room in Rayville. A guy that we knew came in and said, "Have you heard the news? Saddam Hussein has lined up 30,000 troops on Iraq's border with Kuwait."

What in thunder? Next thing we knew they had invaded! Things were starting to get scary. The Sudan, Saddam's ally, lay directly across the Red Sea from Jeddah, and they were threatening to shoot Scud missiles right over our heads. Time to leave!

Barcelona

In haste, I sent my résumé to the State Department in Washington, D.C. They responded that a job was available at the Institute of North American Studies in Barcelona. With that in mind, we packed up all our stuff and had it shipped to Spain. We got on the plane… and went!

The best thing about Barcelona was that Willy was born there. Outside our apartment on National Hwy II stood three Magi; lightning struck at even intervals in the Mediterranean; Willy rode in his Mothercare baby coach.

The Institute (as had been the Raytheon program, to a degree) was modeled on the Peace Corps system, of which many of the teachers were alumni. That meant a hierarchy of coordinators and underlings, most of whom were lesser qualified than I, so it was a humiliating experience. Not only that, but they adhered doggedly to a set of textbooks written by one of their "stars" (who had by that time moved on to bigger and better things), even to the point of writing supplements that only provided more of the same drivel. Two years of that was enough.

Saudi Arabia (Phase 2)

I applied to the Ministry of Health in Saudi Arabia. They had openings, but their consulate in Spain was not able to process my application. We went back to San Francisco for a while, until finally the embassy in Washington, D.C. effectuated the application. That was no easy task, and without their help, no one would have been able to figure out what to do.

First, we had to get all our vital documents (birth certificates, marriage certificates, etc.) notarized. That was not a problem in and of itself; in fact, it was somewhat interesting. In City Hall (San Francisco) there was a civil wedding taking place, complete with the traditional throwing of rice on the bride and groom. Next, we had to march down the street to the office of the Secretary of State (the State of California, not the national government). This took about a week to process, but when that week passed, we went back and received our vital documents, all stamped, sealed and embossed in beautiful gold! The gold was probably what swayed the government of Saudi Arabia.

Anyway, when it came time for us to leave, it was… the Storm of the Century! The entire East Coast was shut down. Our plane was delayed for several days. We transferred flights in North Carolina, marveling at the people's green eyes.

We finally arrived in Riyadh. This time, it was… Hajj! A national holiday when people from around the world go to Mecca to march around the Stone. The whole country was closed. Oh, well, what to do? Wait. After a week we were on our way to Abha, a city on a dead volcano, in the southwest corner of Saudi Arabia, near the Silk Road city of Khamis Mushayt.

Abha.

What was it like, living on top of a dead volcano? Well, the only good volcano is a dead volcano. Troupes of baboons patrolled the escarpment, sometimes doing "electrician work" on the boxes outside of the hospital. (I worked in the Asir Hospital, where we also lived in the housing compound.) On weekends we could walk into town or take a car into Khamis Mushayt to go shopping or stroll around the *souk* (an old-style market).

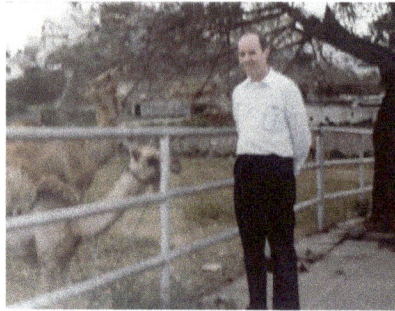

Hillary went to school in the American school, which was mainly for military personnel. At first it was in a little forest, up by where Mr. Mushabob lived. Then they moved it inside the Saudi Air Base, which was a bit of a security problem. In order to pick her up, we would have to first pass the Saudi security checkpoint, then later, the American B-1 bomber base checkpoint.

Japan (Phase 2)

In 1996 we came back to Japan. There were reasons for this. First and foremost was the issue of Hillary's schooling. The Ministry of Health was not too keen on paying for a girl's education, for one. For another, the elementary school in Riyadh only went up to the sixth grade; children wishing to continue to seventh grade would have to go to a boarding school. Time to pack up and leave... again!

My first job was teaching at Fukuoka University. In the meantime, I took a position at Fukuoka Jo Gakuin College in Ogori, but it was a rather long drive. When I was hired full-time at Chikushi, the time schedule did not fit, so I had to quit Fukujo.

It was during this time that I wrote a series of four novels, starting with *The War of Mirrors*. Coming down the steps from my office (there were 65 steps), I noticed a student sitting in the school bus, looking at her mirror and applying makeup from her compact. She saw herself as she wanted to see her, but what did others think when they saw her? Next, I wrote *The Lyre Birds*, a more or less autobiographical novel, and its companion tome, *The Wayfaring Dolphin*. Finally, I wrote *The Bow of Burning Gold*, a story of Saint George and the dragon.

Evening Thoughts

I had a strange upbringing, as the son of a public-school music teacher. As such, I had planned to follow in my father's footsteps; I guess this was my way of paying respect to my father and gaining his approval. But it was not "me."

Instead, I became a private school English teacher. My motto is *eigo ergo sum* ("English, therefore I am"). And so I have lived my life.

I had a kind of "bucket list" (things to do before you "kick the bucket"). Chikushi Jo Gakuen would provide a substantial amount of money if I went to an international conference, so during the last three years before I retired ('15, '16, '17... '18) I went.

The first trip was to Toronto, whence Misa and I took a boat ride under Niagara Falls. It was a kind of Baptism by Nature for me. On to New York, we went to the new Yankee Stadium in the Bronx. I had never been to a live baseball game before that.

The second trip was to San Francisco, though we stayed in Walnut Creek. We went to Chez Panisse in Berkeley, the original Alice's Restaurant. Candlestick park was defunct, but we enjoyed more baseball at ATT (and nearly froze, even in summer).

The third trip was to Boston (sorry, Hannah, but I didn't know you were buried there). Fenway park ultimately satisfied my yearning for baseball. Though it rained throughout, we were safely seated under the roof.

One of the saddest things I have ever experienced was after my father's funeral. Of course, *during* his funeral was sad, but it was offset a bit by the embarrassing spectacle of my uncle, who forgot the words to "Amazing Grace." Afterwards, I strolled through Oakdale Cemetery and came to the children's section. The epitaphs for those dear departed little ones were so touching... I couldn't imagine the grief of their parents... hopes shattered. (The L.A. Board of Supervisors planted a tree in memory of my father when he passed away.)

Some of my happiest memories are these: in 1983 Misa and I were married at Carmel-by-the-Sea; a year later, Hillary was born at Noma-four-square, Japan; in 1991, Willy was born in Barcelona, Spain.

Growing up in a "music" household, I naturally liked music. When I was about sixteen, a sea change came about. The Beatles were to music as "I + 1" is to foreign language teaching. What I mean is, the status quo was always being shaken by something radically different, and that new something eventually became the status quo, until another radically different something came along and shattered the new status quo, and on and on. Each time B. Mitchell Reed, my favorite announcer on KFWB, would say, "…and that was the newest release by the Beatles."

My friend and I wanted to see what all the fuss was about, so we went to Dodger Stadium to see the Beatles. We could hardly hear for all the screaming, but I must say, it was a memorable experience. In the end, though, it was only rock 'n' roll.

Sometimes they have live music at Canal City. One of my fondest memories is of a young Japanese girl playing a folk song on her guitar. It was the sweetest song I have ever heard. I will never know who she was or the name of the song, but that is just fine with me. In this age of "got-to-put-everything-on-facebook," a bit of transience and a bit of time simply spent passing is one of the best things that can happen to a cluttered soul.

Here are the words to a song that I wrote:

The River of Time

Oh, give me fennel and give me dill,
I'll sing a song of the whip-poor-will.
Oh, give me parsley and give me sage,
I'll sing of a long-forgotten age.
I wish I was a youth again,
For I've spent my time and I've spent my wage
On a pint and a bite at the Lion's Den.

Oh, mighty knights of lark and wood,
Who knew what was bad, and what was good.
Oh, pretty ladies who once extolled
The flower of youth, its petals gold.
Don't count the days, don't count the hours,
For the young men one by one grow old,
And the River of Time all things devours.

Well, I hate to say it, but our time on earth does have its limits. If any among you happens to be present at my final curtain call, I would appreciate it if you would play Jeremiah Clarke's "Trumpet Voluntary," as performed by the Compass Rose Orchestra.

164

Afterword

I hope you have enjoyed my little romp, which has spanned both the time and the space occupied by the Stewarts on planet Earth. In writing these narratives, I have always tried to adhere as closely to the truth of the matter as possible. Yes, I have embellished the stories here and there, in cases where the evidence was fuzzy or nonexistent. All in all, the information I have included is correct. If you don't believe me, check it for yourself. (A hex upon those who with malice disparage this tome.)

The Internet is replete with knowledge, but its contents must be taken with a grain of salt (… or a salt *lick*, in some cases). Sometimes it can be a tangle of misinformation. There is one site, for example, which lists Dr. John's father as "Alexander, 5th Earl of Moray," with several other titles added to his name for good measure. While this person's birth year is the same (1634) as the Alexander I have written about, and it sounds glamorous, one should not sacrifice credibility for one small moment of glory; there is greater glory going further back in time. (Why would Earl Moray give up his nice castle and title to go to New England to work as a tailor, anyway?) Plymouth Colony, Massachusetts Bay, New Amsterdam, Jamestown… what more could one hope for in reconstructing his past?

While the Internet can provide a handy tool in spite of its shortcomings, I have tried to use original sources as much as possible. In some cases, I have included persons who are not in fact related to the Stewarts, for the purpose of establishing links to the past. Abraham Temple is included in my anthology because the Templars cannot be traced prior to their arrival in the colonies, whereas the Temples can be traced all the way back to the "Templar" origins of their family. It is a roundabout method, but it works just as well as in the case of the Stewarts, whether we descend through the Lorns, the Appins, the Invernahyles, or the Lairds of Grantully. All are descended from Flaald, the original Seneschal of Dol.

As for Part 2, where I trace our roots back to the Garden of Eden, my research may be met with scholastic skepticism. That I grant you. After all, trying to trace one's ancestry all the way back to the beginning of Man is a very audacious thing to do. Yet all those people existed, did they not? They led real lives in real places at real times, though we do not always have a complete record of them. May they not be forgotten.

As for Part 3, I admit that I have a propensity for playing with numbers. This led me to investigate the seemingly infinite number of theoretical ancestors, if one uses the accepted mathematical formula based on exponents of two.

This exercise of "reliving" people's lives has been invigorating, to say the least. It has also made me feel rather special, though not unique. If everybody were to delve into his or her past, what jewels might they find? Of course, there may be some who say to themselves, "I'm just

165

some clod; I can trace my roots all the way back to my grandfather, who was also just some clod." Be of good cheer, boys and girls. Even if you cannot find the evidence, the facts are still there: we all trace our roots back through Noah to Adam and Eve. That makes you, even the lowliest clod, someone special! Your life matters!

Reading my mother's and my father's books was a somewhat sad, though informative, experience. Some of those events I had lived through myself, yet my parents saw what happened from a different perspective. I had a feeling of desolation while reading, probably because I never liked Texas very much, Oklahoma even less. My parents ended up in California, which I liked but ultimately felt the need to leave. Reading about their lives left me feeling somewhat empty, yet their *persons* made me full: I thought they were saints, in every sense of the word.

Now it is time to say farewell. I will end with the words from my mother's book: "Be ever thankful that you will not have to suffer the way those who came before you did! Always remember it was done so you could have a better life!"

God bless you, and Godspeed.

Jan Eylander Jackson Stewart
Laird of Glen Coe and Lochaber
December 2020

Part 3
How Many Ancestors do I Have?

Exploring the Wind Chime Model of Genealogy Studies

"That in blessing I will bless thee, and in multiplying I will multiply thy seed as the stars of the heaven, and as the sand which *is upon* the sea shore; and thy seed shall possess the gate of his enemies…"

… Genesis 22.17 (KJV)

The books written by my mother and father contain appendices with genealogy charts going back several generations, as far as they could trace them using the tools they had at their disposal. Reading those charts is a dizzying experience: they don't all fit onto one page, so you have to follow seemingly endless lines of offspring and husbands and wives to keep track of "who's who in the past," so to speak. There must be an easier way.

As I looked at all those charts, I thought to myself that if I could trace them all the way back to the beginning (!), there would surely be millions of ancestors lining my past. I began to calculate, based on the standard formula:

$$\text{for n generations, Ancestors} = 2^{(n+1)} - 2 \text{ (for Adam \& Eve)}.$$

However, the "plus one" seems to be redundant, given the "minus two" for Adam and Eve, so for the purposes of this study I will use a simple mathematical formula:

$$\text{for n generations, Ancestors} = 2^{(n-1)}.$$

In other words, in the second generation, I have 2 parents. In the third, I have 4 grandparents. In the fourth, I have 8 great-grandparents, and so on. And so on?

How many generations am I from the beginning? One study shows that the British Royal Family trace their lineage back through the Kings of England, beginning with James I (14 generations), the Kings of Scotland (25 generations), the Kings of Argyll in northern Scotland (13 generations), the Kings of Ireland (54 generations), the Kings of Israel/Judah (18 generations), the Post-Diluvian Kings (23 generations), and the Ante-Diluvian Kings (9 generations): a total of 158 generations to Prince George (see Appendix 3). As I am nearly an exact contemporary of Prince Charles (George's grandfather), I can reckon myself to be approximately 156 generations from Adam. The formula gives us an impossible number of ancestors:

$$2^{156-1} =$$

$$4,5671,926,166,590,716,193,865,151,022,383,844,364,247,891,968$$

$$\text{or} = 4.5 \times 10^{45}$$

How can this be? Most estimates of the TOTAL number of people who have ever lived on earth are in the range of 108 billion! The exponential figure derived above must be wildly exaggerated! To solve this strange but imminently practical mathematical problem, let us examine a more manageable segment of the human population – all the generations from Adam to Noah.

Noah was the tenth generation from Adam. Therefore, according to our formula, he should have had 512 ancestors (2^9). However, if we look at Table 1 below, we can see that in many instances Noah's ancestors married their sisters or their cousins, increasing the chances that they would have *shared* ancestors, and reducing the total number of Noah's (and our) ancestors.

Instead of 512 ancestors, we see from the chart that Noah had only 23 known ancestors. Add these together with the "question mark" spouses, which make 28 ancestors. Thus, Noah's ten generations can be grouped together into a "wind chime," that is, a closely knit group of people – a tribe – who intermarry, only occasionally breaking the pattern to marry into another tribe.

In the case of Noah's sons (Shem, Ham, Japheth), the number of ancestors increases significantly, because their mother Na'amah came from a different "wind chime" – the line of Cain (it is ironic that the line of Cain is continued through Na'amah). If the pattern of intra-tribal marriage in that family was similar to that of Noah, then Shem, Ham and Japheth would probably have double the number of ancestors as their father Noah: 56.

Table 1. Descendants of Adam and Eve.

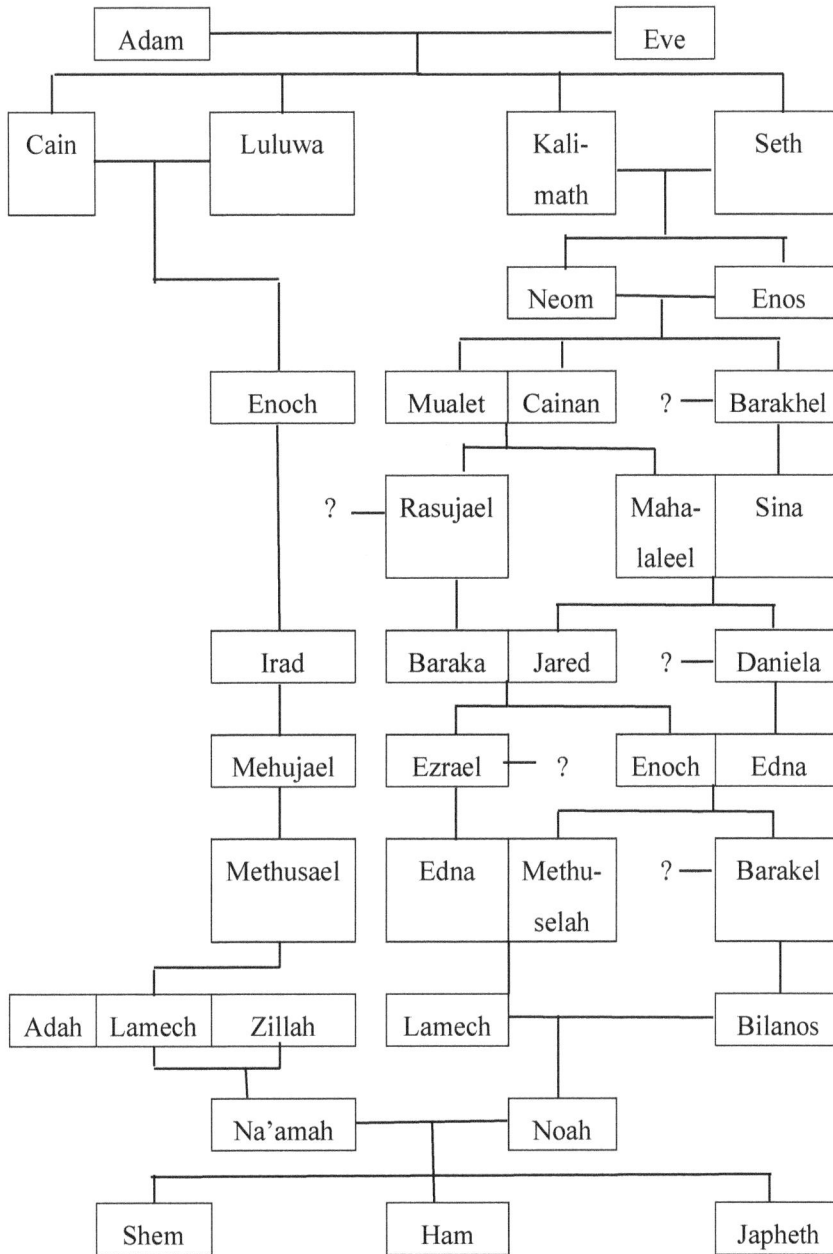

Genesis 4:1-22   Genesis 4:25-32

Granted, there is a lot we do not know about those original ancestors of Shem, Ham and Japheth. It was likely that the line of Cain was *anathema* to the line of Seth, so inter-marriage was frowned upon. However, the model that arises from intra-clan marriage tends to limit the number of ancestors that any one person might have. They lived in a closed system.

In an open system, things are much different. According to our (simplified) mathematical model, we can see the following hypothetical ancestry chart, of Xs and Ys, in an open system:

Table 2. A five-generation genealogy chart.

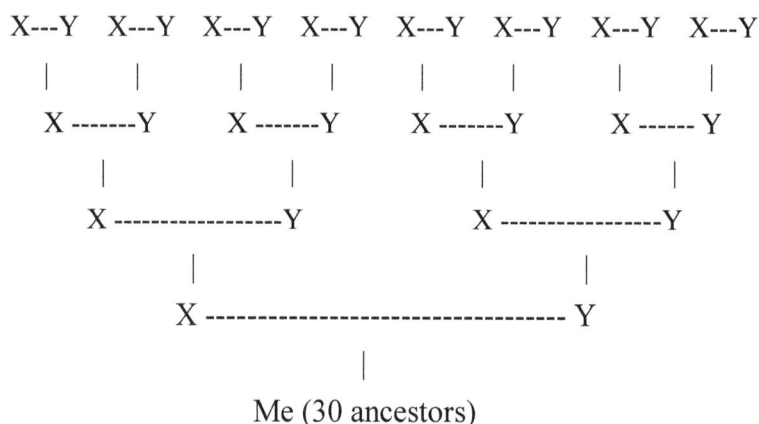

```
X---Y   X---Y   X---Y   X---Y   X---Y   X---Y   X---Y   X---Y
  |       |       |       |       |       |       |       |
  X -------Y       X -------Y       X -------Y       X ------ Y
    |               |               |               |
    X -----------------Y           X -----------------Y
        |                               |
        X -------------------------------- Y
                        |
                Me (30 ancestors)
```

In this scheme, it took me only four generations to chalk up more ancestors than Noah did in nine generations! Over the course of *twelve* generations, one would have 4,096 ancestors. (If you use this model for twenty generations, you will have more than a million ancestors!) I will use this figure (4,096) throughout the following discussion.

The Wind-Chime Model: A Longitudinal Study

Table 1 above illustrates the wind-chime model in a tightly knit society. This could only be possible under the conditions that the Patriarchs experienced. Control was maximized. Population was minimal. As time went on, however, and population increased, control began to slip away, and extra-tribal marriage became more commonplace.

Anthropologists tell us that early peoples were hunter-gatherers, only evolving into farmers about 8,000 years ago. However, Genesis tells us that already in the second generation (Cain), people were tilling the soil. That makes for a fairly "grounded" society. In addition, sheepherders (such as Abel) are by no means nomads; they keep to a well-defined territory, tending not to stray, for fear of wolves (or their murderous brothers). For the sake of example, I will consider a rather sedentary, theoretical population of farmers and herders over many, many generations, to illustrate the windchime model.

Given the physical limitations of farming, and the presumed lack of efficient transportation, early people most likely grouped themselves into tribes, or other social units. Marriage within one's tribe would have been preferred, but occasionally a person might venture outside that group and marry into another tribe. Nearby tribes would be the most likely destination:

Table 3. Neighboring Tribes.

Tribe A	Tribe B	Tribe C
Tribe D	Tribe E	Tribe F
Tribe G	Tribe H	Tribe I

Over twelve generations, marriage within one's tribe would produce 4,096 members. However, if a person married *outside* his or her tribe, that would effectively double the number of ancestors, depending on which generation he belonged to. Not knowing that precise information, we might be able to average the number to 2,048 (the eleven-generation mark) for any tribe in which the marriage took place. Within these neighboring nine tribes, therefore, we may calculate that over twelve generations a person would have 18,432 potential ancestors.

Table 4. The wind-chime model.

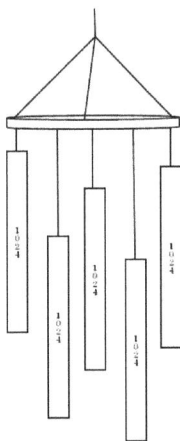

Returning to our earlier mathematical model, we have seen what can happen (in an open system) over one hundred fifty-six generations! With this new wind-chime model, we are able to expand our twelve-generation estimate thirteen times (12 x 13 = 156 generations). We may then calculate a new (theoretical) number of ancestors: 13 x 18,432 = 239,616. This model allows for inter-tribal marriage, considering an average number of ancestors for each twelve generations, but also accounting for the number of *shared* ancestors that tribal societies would possibly produce.

171

Now let us move on to the area from which many of my ancestors came – Scotland and Ireland. Among the first settlers to the region were the colonists of the Milesian migration.* Assuming that these 150 colonists became farmers or herders, it behooves us to know how many people the land could support, at most.

A "hide" (120 acres) was the measure of land that was necessary to support a farmer and his family for a year. (Forests and mountains are suitable for hunting.) Here are some statistics:

Scotland =

    7,800,000 hectares divided by 100 = 78,000 hunter-gatherers;

    5.7 million hectares = 14,085,007 acres of arable land;

    14,085,007 acres divided by 120 = 117,375 farming families.

Ireland =

    6,900,000 hectares divided by 100 = 69,000 hunter-gatherers;

    4.5 million hectares = 11,119,742 acres of arable land;

    11,119,742 divided by 120 = 92,664 farming families.

The Irish Genealogies list no fewer than 139 clans, or family groups, which existed in ancient Ireland. Although we do not know the exact size of these clans, their average numbers can be deduced by dividing a population of roughly 740,000 (assuming each family had eight members**) by 140 (taking into consideration possibly one missing clan), which results in an average of 5,300 members for each clan. If it takes 15 acres of farmland to support each person, then one clan would require an area of nearly 75,000 acres (approximately 10 miles square) to support life. If we think about the physical limitations of inter-clan marriage, we see an interesting trend:

* These came from Spain after 1699 B.C.. Milesius was the 36th generation from Adam, a contemporary of Solomon.

** People in those days tended to have seven or eight children, some of whom may not have lived to adulthood. In Ireland, 92,000 families x 8 members each = 736,000 population.

Table 5. An Irish Example

Clan A O'Toole	Clan B Connor	Clan C Riley
Clan D Duffy	Clan E Meller	Clan F Flynn
Clan G Quinn	Clan H Ryan	Clan I Kelly

If members of Clan E (Meller) marry within their own clan according to the "wind chime" model, as seen in Noah's ancestry, they may share the same ancestors 25 out of 28 times over a course of twelve generations. A person seeking a marriage partner from a different clan may have to look five to ten miles away to find a husband/wife.

Moreover, in any one generation, the number of eligible marriage partners (those within five years of age of any given person) would be about one-fifth of the total population. In a clan of 5,300 persons, this would be 1,060 persons, of whom 530 would be of the opposite sex. In the total cluster represented by Clans A-I in Table 5, the total persons who would be possible spouses would be 530 x 9 = 4,770 per generation. Over a period of twelve generations, the total would be 57,240. From Adam to Edward, Duke of Kent (contemporary with my Irish ancestor, John W. Milor) there are one hundred fifty generations, or 12.5 windchime cycles. Therefore, the total of *possible* ancestors (limited to the geographical area occupied by Clans A-I) would be 12.5 x 57,240 = 715,500 persons. Of course, this is a very conservative average estimate. The actual number may have been much different.

Europe

In the Grand Scheme of Things, Scotland and Ireland play their parts, but there is more than meets the eye. After the Flood, descendants of Noah began to migrate to the far reaches of the earth. In the course of this migration, we can trace our roots back to two of Noah's sons, Shem and Japheth.

Japheth's descendants Gomer and Magog went northward, into Europe. Gomer, then, would be the patriarch of the Angles, Saxons and Jutes who colonized England, and eventually Scotland. Magog, on the other hand, went into Scythia. Milesius (generation #36) then reversed this trend and went into Spain. From there he led the most long-lasting colonization of Ireland, driving out the Tuatha da Danaan and other early inhabitants.

Table 6. Ancestors of Europe and the British Isles.

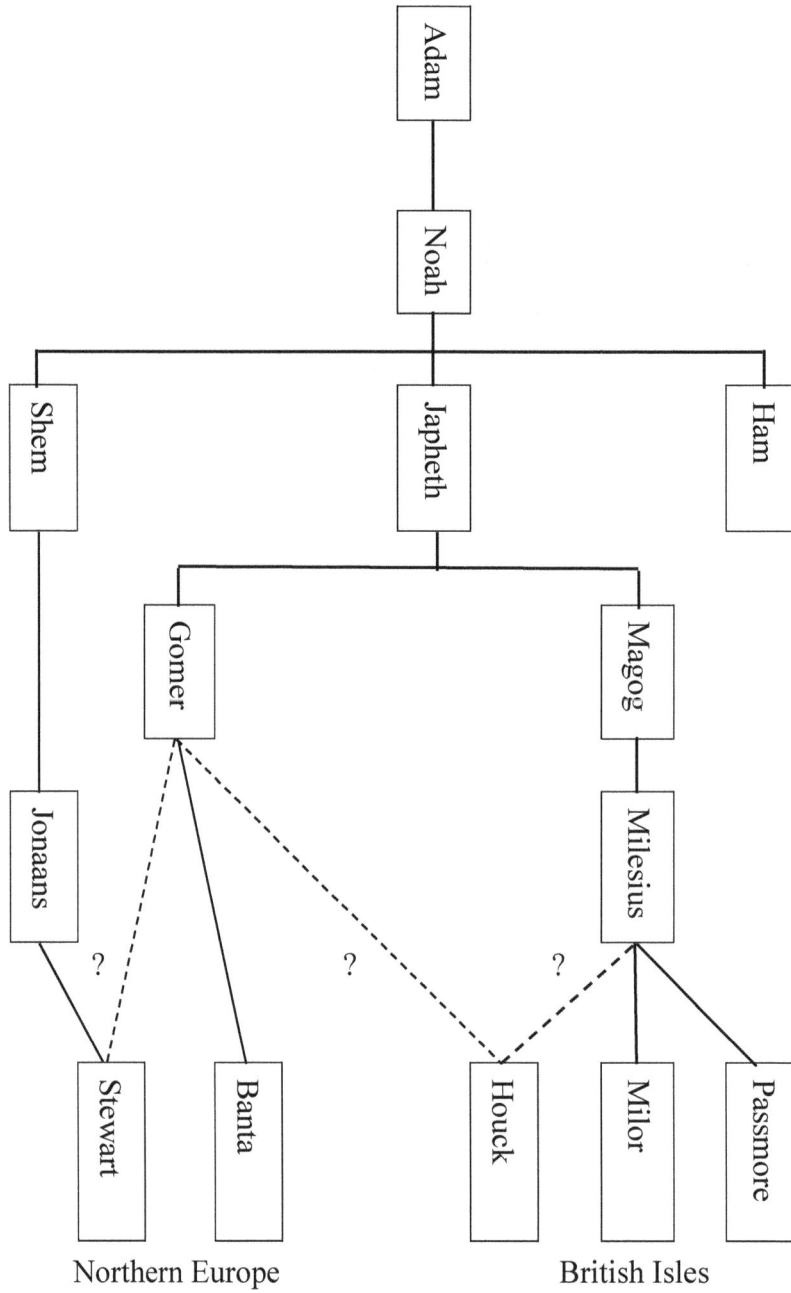

North America

In the case of immigrants to North America, the resulting demographic would constitute a limited open system. It was *limited* in the sense that most (though not all) marriages took place among English speakers; none involved non-European descendants. It was *open* in the sense that a mobile society eliminated the windchime effect.

In most cases (Banta, Passmore, Alberti), I am an eleventh-generation American. I am a tenth-generation Stewart, and a fifth generation Milor (see Table 7, below). I am a one hundred fifty-sixth generation son of Adam.* For the most part, then, there were twelve cycles of twelve generations that lived before the great migration to North America, after which ten or eleven generations fanned out in a migratory pattern in an open system.

Conclusion

According to the data I have hitherto laid out, the twelve-generation windchime cycle serves as a reasonable model for ancestry study, over a course of twelve cycles (144 generations). We have seen that in a very closed system such as that of Noah, its average of 2,048 ancestors per cycle is greatly overstated, but over several cycles, the additive nature of the windchime model accounts for the phenomenon of shared ancestry much more efficiently than does the mathematical (exponential) model.

In my own case, the issue of shared ancestors becomes readily apparent. My mother's father's mother's maiden name was Stewart. There have been several other instances, among my progenitors, of men marrying women having the same surname as their ancestors. Moreover, my great-great grandfather "Old" John Banta married a woman named McDonald, whose ancestors ultimately trace their roots back to Margaret Stewart, scion of the original High Stewards of Scotland. Such instances greatly reduce the number of my ancestors.

Twelve cycles, according to the additive longitudinal windchime model, produces 12 x 2,048 = 24,576 ancestors. Multiply this by five-and-a-half "windchime" lines (Stewart + shared Stewart, Passmore, Milor, Banta, Houck) and you get 5.5 x 24,576 = 135,168 ancestors over twelve cycles. Add to that the eleven generations using the exponential formula for the North American open system, and you get the total number of ancestors for me: 135,168 + 2,048 = 137,216 ancestors. This is a very conservative estimate, so we may consider it as a "minimum" number.

In the above cross-sectional study, the maximum number of ancestors for 144 generations x 530 eligible spouses x 9 nearby clans x 5.5 "chimes" = 3,777,840 + 2,048 (N. American open system) = 3,779,888 ancestors. Consider this a "maximum" number of ancestors.

* Other reckonings show my case to be "only" 122 generations.

Table 7. North American Exponential Model

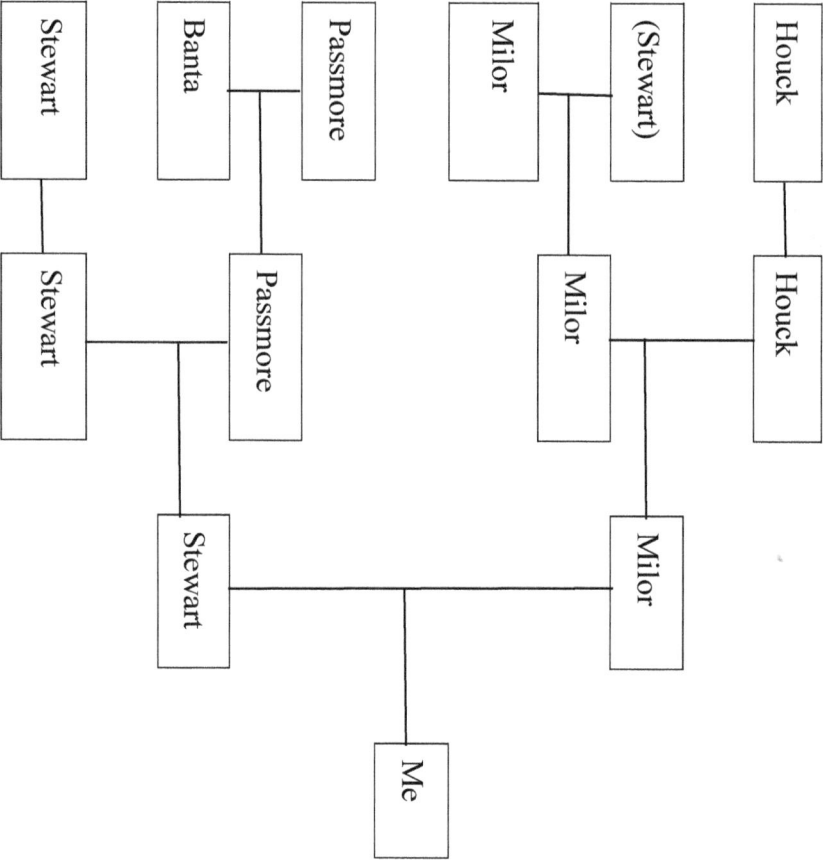

Incidentally, these numbers are *not* more than all the stars in the heavens, nor all the grains of sand on the seashore. Estimates of the former are something on the order of 1×10^{24}; of the latter, 5.6×10^{21}. The exponential model used by most genealogists today renders a number that would be roughly the number of stars *times* the number of grains of sand (2.8×10^{45}), a figure which is clearly impossible, given the estimated total number of people (1.08×10^{11}) that have occupied the earth since the beginning.

In answer to the question, "How many ancestors do I have?" the additive "windchime" system offers a much more realistic estimate than the totally unrealistic model of the traditional, exponential formula used by many students of genealogy today. The "windchime" number would lie somewhere between the minimum (137,216) and the maximum (3,779,888). And I may safely say that they are fewer than the stars of the heaven, or the grains of sand on the seashore.

References

Garber, Megan, "How Many Stars Are There in the Sky?"
The Atlantic, November 19, 2013.

Marshall, Jason, "How Many Grains of Sand Are on Earth's Beaches?"
Scientific American, August 29, 2012.

Appendix 1 –
New Amsterdam

Directions to Pietro Alberti's House, 1638 (circled in blue).

Directions to Epke Jacobse's House, 1659 (circled in red).

Manhattan in 1600, compared to Manhattan today.

Appendix 2-

"The Bonnie Earl O'Moray"

In 1592, King James VI commissioned the Earl of Huntly to hunt down the Earl of Moray (husband of Elizabeth, the king's cousin). He tracked him down, but the Earl of Moray would not surrender. The house in which he was hiding was set on fire, and the Earl of Moray was killed. During the fracas, Huntly gashed his face. "You have spoiled a better face than your own," said the dying Earl of Moray. The Morays were the hereditary keepers of Doune castle in Perthshire.

This song commemorates James Stewart, #110 of the "High Road," listed on page 49 above.

Ye Hielan's an' ye Lowlan's
O, where have ye been?
They hae slain the Earl of Moray
And lain him on the green.
He was a braw gallant
And he rode at the ring.
An' the bonnie Earl of Moray
O, he micht hae been the king!
O, lang may his lady
Look frae the castle Doune,
Ere she see the Earl of Moray
Come soundin' through the toun.

Now way be to thee, Huntly
And wherefore did ye sae?
I bade you bring him wi' you
But forbade you him to slay.
He was a braw gallant
And he play'd at the ball
An' the Bonnie Earl of Moray
Was a flower among them all.

Lang may his lady
Look from the Castle Doune,
Ere she see the Earl of Moray
Come soundin' through the toun.

Ye Hielan's and ye Lowlan's
O where hae ye been?
They have slain the Earl of Moray
An' laid him on the green.
He was a braw gallant
And he rode at the gluve
An' the Bonnie Earl of Moray
O, he was the Queens' true love.
Lang will his lady
Look frae the Castle Doune,
Ere she see the Earl of Moray
Come soundin' through the toun.

The Bonnie Earl O'Moray

In 1954, *Harper's Magazine* published an article by Sylvia Wright, who confessed that she had misheard the words "And layed him on the green," believing they had killed the Earl O'Moray along with his lover, Lady Mondegreen. The term "mondegreen" is now commonly used for any misheard song lyric that changes the original meaning.

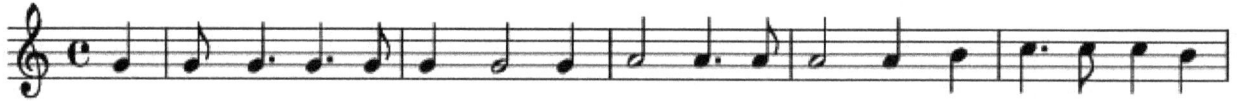

Ye Hie- lands an' ye Law- lands, Oh where hae ye been? They have slain the Earl o'

Mur- ray. And layed him on the green. He was a braw gal- lant And he rade a' the

ring, And the bon- ny Earl o' Mur- ray, He might hae been a king!

Sir John Stewart (1687-1764) was the 15th Laird of Grantully and 3rd Baronet. He descended from William Steuart, 9th of Grantully, and a second wife Isobel (née) Stewart. Sir John married Lady Jane Douglas.

Sir John Stewart of Grandtully's Strathspey [1]

Appendix 3 –
The British Royal Family (and others)

Ham	Shem Genesis 5:1-32	Japheth (libraryireland.com)
	1 Adam 4000-3070 BC	
	2 Seth	
	3 Enos	
	4 Cainan	
	5 Mahalaleel	
	6 Jared	
	7 Enoch	
	8 Methuselah	
	9 Lamech	
	10 Noah 2943-2007 BC	
11 Ham	11 Shem	11 Japheth
	12 Arphaxad Gen. 11:10-26	12 Magog (+ Gomer)
	13 Salah*	13 Baoth, King of Scythia
	14 Eber	14 Fenius Farsaidh, King of Scythia
	15 Peleg	15 Niul Nemnach
	16 Reu	16 Gaodhal Glas
	17 Serug	17 Asruth
	18 Nahor	18 Sruth
	19 Terah	19 Heber Scutt
	20 Abram /Abraham 1992--1917	20 Beouman
	21 Isaac	21 Oghaman, King of Scythia
	22 Jacob	22 Tait, King of Scythia

(Old Testament Spellings)

* Luke 3:36 inserts Cainan as the father of Salah.

Ham	Shem Luke 3:31-38	Japheth libraryireland
	23 Judah b. 1752 BC Gen 29.35	23 Agnan
	24 Phares	24 Lamhfionn
	25 Ezrom	25 Heber Glunfionn
	26 Aram	26 Agnan Fionn
	27 Aminadab	27 Febric Glas
	28 Naasson	28 Nenuall
	29 Salmon	29 Nuadhad
	30 Boaz 1312 BC	30 Alladh
	31 Obed	31 Arcadh
	32 Jesse	32 Deagh
	Kings of Israel / Judah:	
	33 King David 1085-1015 BC	33 Brath
	34 King Solomon	34 Breoghan
	35 King Roboam	35 Bile
	36 King Abia	36 Milesius of Spain
	37 King Asa	m. Scota Tephi
	38 King Josaphat	37 King Heremon
	39 King Joram m. Athaliah	
	40 King Ozias m. Zibiah	
	41 King Joatham m. Jehoaddan	
	42 King Achaz m. Jecholiah	
	43 King Ezekias m. Jerusha	
	44 King Jotham	
	45 King Ahaz m. Abi	
	46 King Hezekiah m. Hephzibah	
	47 King Manasseh m. Meshallemeth	
	48 King Amon 621-641 m. Jedidiah	
	49 King Josiah 649-610 m. Mamutah	
	50 King Zedekiah r. 599-578 BC	

(New Testament Spellings)

Jesusevidence.com	Jesusevidence.com	Jesusevidence.com
51 Queen Tea Tephi* b. 565 BC	75 King Jaran Gleofathach	97 King Caibre Liffeachair
m. #37 King Heremon	76 King Coula Cruaidh Cealgach	r. 267-284 AD
52 King Irial Faidh	77 King Oiliolla Caisfhiachach	98 King Fiachadh Sreabthuine
53 King Eithriall	78 King Eochaidh Foltleathan	99 King Muireadhach Tireach
54 Follain	79 King Aongns Tuirmheach	100 King Eochaidh Moigmeodhin
55 King Tighernmas	Teamharch 384-324 BC	101 King Nail of the 9 Hostages
56 Eanbotha	80 King Eana Aighneach	102 Eogan
57 Smiorguil	r. 312-292 BC	103 King Murireadhach
58 King Fiachadh Labhri	81 Labhra Suire	104 Earca
59 King Aongus Ollmuch	82 Blathucha	
60 Maoin	83 Easamhuin Famhua	Kings of Argyll:
61 King Rotheachta	84 Roighnein Ruadh	105 King Fergus More d. 501
62 Dein	85 Finlogha	106 King Dongard
63 King Siorna Saoghalach	86 Fian	107 King Conran
64 Oholla Olchaoin	87 King Eodchaidh Feidhlioch	108 King Aidan
65 King Giallchadh	r. 142-130 BC	109 King Eugene IV
66 King Aodhain Glas	88 Fineamhuas	110 King Donald IV
67 Simeon Breac	89 King Lughaidh Raidhdearg	111 Dongard
68 Muirteadach Bolgrach	90 King Criomhthan Niadhnar	112 King Eugene V
69 Fiachadh Toigrach	r. 7-9 AD	113 Findan
70 Duach Laidhrach	91 Fearaidhach Fion Feachtnuigh	114 King Eugene VII
71 Eochaidh Bualgllerg	92 King Fiachadh Fionoluidh	115 King Etfinus
72 Ugaine More the Great	93 King Tuathal Teachtmar	116 King Achaius
73 Cobhthach Coalbreag	94 King Coun Ceadchathach	117 King Alpin d. 834
r. 591-451 BC	95 King Arb Aonflier	
74 Meilage	96 King Cormae Usada	

* Author's Note: Some scholars doubt the existence of Tea Tephi. However, it is possible that a child of Zedekiah came to Ireland from Egypt by way of Spain during the Milesian migration. Tea is said to be the daughter of *Lughaidh*, which in Irish means "God's House." She could have been a ward of the house of Pharaoh who came to Spain with her sister Scota. It would be understandable if the British Royal Family wanted to downplay its direct descent from Magog through Heremon.

Jesusevidence.com	Jesusevidence.com	Jesusevidence.com
Kings of Scotland:	133 Robert Bruce I 1274-1329	145 Princess Sophia of Hanover
118 King Kenneth I d 858	m. Isobel of Mar	m. Duke Ernest of Brunswick
119 King Constantin I d. 878	134 Marjorie Bruce 1296-1316	146 King George I 1660-1727
120 King Donald II d. 900	m. **Walter Stewart III**	m. Sophia Dorothea of Celle
121 King Malcom I d. 954	dtr Margaret m. John MacD.	147 King George II 1683-1760
122 King Kenneth II d. 995	135 King Robert II Stewart d. 1390	m. Pr. Caroline of Brandenburg
123 King Malcom II d. 1034	m. Euphemia of Ross	148 Prince Frederick Lewis Wales
124 Bethoc (daughter)	136 King Robert III 1337-1406	m. Pr. Augusta of Saxe-Gotha
m. Abbot Crinan	m. Annabella Drummond	149 King George III 1738-1820
125 King Duncan I d. 1040	137 James I Scotland 1394-1437	m. Pr. Sophia of Mecklenburgh
m. Sybil	m. Joan Beaufort	150 Duke Edward of Kent
126 King Malcolm III d. 1093	138 James II Scotland 1430-1460	m. Pr. Victoria of Saxe-Coburg
m. Margaret of Wessex	m. Mary of Gueldres	(1816~**J. Wm. Milor**)
127 King David I 1084-1153	139 James III Scotland 1451-1488	151 Queen Victoria 1819-1901
m. Matilda of Huntingdon	m. Pr. Margarct of Denmark	m. Pr. Albert of Saxe-Coburg
128 Prince Henry 1114-1152	140 James IV Scotland 1473-1513	152 King Edward VII 1841-1910
m. Ada of Surrey	m. Margaret of England	m. Princess Alexandra
129 Earl David 1152-1219	141 James V Scotland 1512-1542	153 King George V 1865-1936
m. Matilda of Chester	m. Mary of Lorraine	m. Princess Mary of Teck
130 Isobel of Huntingdon	142 Mary Q of Scots 1542-1587	154 King George VI 1895-1952
m. Robert Bruce III	m. Lord Henry Darnley	m. Lady Elizabeth Bowes-Lyon
131 Robert Bruce IV 1215-1295	143 James VI Scotland / I England	155 Queen Elizabeth II b. 1926
m. Isobel of Gloucester	m. Anne of Denmark	m. Duke Philip of Edinburgh
132 Robert Bruce V 1243-1304	144 Princess Elizabeth	156 Prince Charles b. 1948
m. Martha of Carrick	m. Frederick V, Elektor Palatine	m. Lady Diana Spencer

Appendix 4 –
The McDonald Connection

The Original "Golden Arches"

John   Margaret
MacDonald   Stewart

King Ivar II of Waterford	Angus MacDonald	Alexander Alasdair MacDonnell
b. Ireland d. 1000	b. 1248 Scotland	b. 1580 (d. Ireland)
Ranald Ivarsson	Angus MacDonald (Lord of Isles)	Sir James Archibald MacDonnell
b. 974 Dublin	b. 1274 Scotland	b. 1615 Ireland
Ranald Ranaldsson	John MacDonald	Sir Daniel MacDonnell
b. Perth, Scotland	b. 1318 Scotland	b. 1640 Ireland
Meargach MacRagnaill	m. Princess Margaret Stewart	Sir John MacDonnell
b. 1010 Dublin	John Mor Tanister MacDonald	b. 1670 Ireland
Solam	b. 1360 Scotland	Sir John Landon McDaniel
b. Dublin	Donald MacDonald	b. 1695 Virginia
Giolla Adhamnan	b. 1407 Scotland	John McDaniel
b. 1065 Scotland	John Mor MacDonald	b. 1720 Virginia
Gillebride MacGille Adomnan	b. 1445 Ireland	John Ely McDonald (McDaniel)
b. 1085 Ireland	Sir John Cathanach MacDonald	b. 1740, Virginia
Somerled MacGillebride	B. 1435 Ireland	Linville McDonald
b. 1115 Scotland	Alexander Carragh MacDonald	b. 1768 North Carolina
Ranald Somerled MacSomahirle	b. 1478 Ireland (Ulster)	Thomas McDonald
b. 1153 Scotland	Somhairle Buidhe MacDonnell	b. 1803 North Carolina
Donald Ragnaldson MacRaghnaill	b. 1505 Ireland	Rebecca Angeline McDonald
b. 1200 Scotland	Sir James MacDonnell	b. 1842 Illinois
	b. 1550 (d. Ireland)	m. **John Walter Banta**

Index of Names

C

Calvin, John	4, 22	Cole, Susanna	2
Campbell, Colin "The Red Fox"	3	Collins, Billy	33 F.N.
Candacy	28 F.N.	Constantine, Emp. (Rome)	31 F.N.
Carver, George Washington	6 F.N.	Copeland, Sarah	6 F.N.
Castell, Carl (Count)	8 F.N.	Corbell, C.A.	29
Cato, Epsey	28	Cornelisda, Coely Sil	23
Cecilia of Dunbar	16	Covington, Virginia	7
Charles I, King (England)	20	Crawford, Eva	13
Charles II, King (England)	23	Cremona, Lady Veronica	22
Cingris, Pharaoh	31	Croesus	29
Clarke, Jeremiah	36	Cromwell, Oliver	1
Cnut, King	19	Custer, Gen. George	33
Cole, John	2	Cynfelyn (Cymbeline)	The Temples

D

David I, King (Scotland)	12, 14	Dirckse, Sitske	23
Davis, Jefferson	25	Dorsey, Jimmy	9
Davis, "Wild" John	7	Dorsey, Tommy	9
Devore, Chuck	10	Donnchad of Mar	13

E

Edward the Confessor	19	Elizabeth de Burgh	17
Edward I, II King(s)	16, 17	Epkese, Cornelius (Egbert)	23
Eleanor, Cherokee	34	Eschina of London	12
Elizabeth I, Queen	5, 24		

J-K

Jackson, Pres. Andrew	28	Jord	18
Jacobse, Epke	10, NY to TX	Joseph of Arimathea	2, The Temples
James, Duke of York	23	Kalberlahn, Hans	4
James, Harry	9	Kennedy, Pres. John F.	6 F.N., 10
James I, King	20	Kieft, Gov. William	2
James, Saint (Apostle)	16 F.N.	King, Martin Luther	6 F.N.
Jarvis, Liz (the Parrot Lady)	10	Kitchner, Polly	5, 6 F.N.
Jefferson, Pres. Thomas	5	Krupa, Gene	9
John the Baptist	19		

L

Landaal, Ruth	10	Leowfine	19
Langtry, Emilie Charlotte	33	Lincoln, Pres. Abraham	27, 28
Lathrop, Jane	2 F.N.	Loki (Araknis)	18
Lawrie, Gawain	23	Londres, Eschina	12
Lee, Sarah	28 F.N.	Louis IX, King (France)	15
Lehmann, Herman	18 F.N.	Luuesz, Epke	23
Leofric, Earl of Mercia	19		

P

Passmore, Alma	30	Passmore, Minnie	8, 26
Passmore, Alexander	27	Passmore, Thomas	27
Passmore, Andrew Jr.	28	Patrick, Saint	31
Passmore, Angie	29	Paulk, Jane	27
Passmore, Daymon	8, 30	Pelles, King	11
Passmore, Dora	30	Philip, Apostle	The Temples
Passmore, George	27	Philip, King (of France)	13
Passmore, Houseman	27	Philip, King (Indian)	1
Passmore, Leah	8, 30	Plato	10
Passmore, Leonard	26, 29	Pritchard, Richard	21

R

Rainwater, Flo	34	Reginald mac Somerled	13
Rainwater, Olen "Chief"	34	Revere, Paul	19
Rankin, Jeannette	9	Richard, King (the Lion-Heart)	13
Reed, B. Mitchell	36		

T

U-W

References

Banta, L.W., *The Banta Blue Book, or a century in Texas with the Banta family.*
NP. 1947.

Banta, Theodore M., *A Frisian Family – The Banta Genealogy.*
New York: 1893. //archive.org/details/frisianfamilyban00bant/

Doubell, Sharon Lee, "Banquo – matrilineal descent options that might link
Banquo to the Stewart line." https: // www geni com/discussions/113421

Family Bible of David Kimbrough Stewart. Purchased 1865.

Heitman, Francis B., *Historical Register of Officers of the
Continental Army during The War of the Revolution.*
Washington DC: The Rare Book Shop Publishing Co., Inc.
1914. https: // archive org / details/franheitmanreg00bernrich

Hoare, Christobel Mary, *Records of a Norfolk Village, Being Notes on the
History of the Parish of Sidestrand.* Bedford: The Beds. Times Publ. Co., Ltd., 1914.

Josselyn, John, *New-England's Rarities Discovered.*
London: G. Widdowes, at the Green Dragon in St. Pauls Church-yard, 1672.

Math Is Fun. (https: // www. mathsisfun.com/calculator-precision.html)

Michell, John, *The Dimensions of Paradise.*
San Francisco: Harper & Row, 1988.

Passmore, Leonard J., *Evening Thoughts, by Babe Bert.*
Edited by Leonard Jackson Stewart. Walnut, Ca, 1983.

Paul, Sir James Balfour (Ed.), *The Scots Peerage*, Vol. 1.
Edinburgh: David Douglas, 1904.

Steel, Richard, *The Evidence for Jesus*. River Harvest Ministries.
Berforts Information Press Ltd., 2015.

Stewart, Faye (Milor-Houck), *"Little Sam."* Walnut, CA, 1981.

Stewart, Faye (Milor-Houck), *A Glance at the Past.* Walnut, CA, 1984.

Stewart, Jan E.J. *Collected Works*. https: // chikushi academia edu / JanStewart

Stewart, John H.J., and Duncan Stewart, *Stewarts of Appin.*
Edinburgh: Machlachlan and Stewart, 1880 (Bodleian Library).

Stewart, Leonard Jackson, *A.J. Passmore.* Walnut, CA, 1983.

Stewart, Leonard Jackson, *My Life in Retrospect.* Walnut, CA., 1983.

Stewart, Leonard Jackson (Ed.), *The Writings of Leonard Passmore.* Walnut, CA, 1984.

Stewart, Leonard Jackson, *Old John Banta – A Biographical Sketch.* Walnut, CA, 1986.

Temple, Dr. Henry Curtis, *The Temple Family in England and America 856 A.D. to 1930 A.D.*
Alliance, Ohio, 1930.

The Forme of Cury (The Method of Cooking), 14th C.

Wyman, Thomas Bellows, *The Genealogies and Estates of Charlestown*, Vol. 1, A-J; Vol. 2, K-Z).
Boston: David Clapp and Son, 1879. Internet Archive.
https: // archive org / details / genealogiesestat02wyma /

www.ingramcontent.com/pod-product-compliance
Lightning Source LLC
Chambersburg PA
CBHW050416110426
42812CB00006BA/1904